MW01289011

Book of Counted Sorrows

Volume II

Volume II

Allen D. Miller

authorHOUSE®

AuthorHouse™
1663 Liberty Drive, Suite 200
Bloomington, IN 47403
www.authorhouse.com
Phone: 1-800-839-8640

First published by AuthorHouse 4/13/2009

ISBN: 978-1-4389-4040-3 (sc)

Printed in the United States of America
Bloomington, Indiana

This book is printed on acid-free paper.

Introduction

In November of 1975, I was discharged from the Army at Ft Bliss, Texas.

At this time I had been working on a series of writings dealing with human nature, feelings and the hearts of people, when different situations arise.

I entitled the writings "The Book of Counted Sorrows", which at that time was approximately 400 pages and had several dedications, and at that point I felt, I wanted to publish these writings.

However, it happened the manuscript was lost, after I copyrighted it in 1977 the first time, and so in 1979 it began again, only with fresh material and some that was recovered here and there.

I now am here to present to you Volume II, but Volume I is not completely lost.

I have a lot of people that have pushed me to go ahead with this and when I do get Volume I underway, I promise you will be surprised at the depth of its content, as well as, the broad spectrum of feeling it covers.

This being published first is Dedicated to foremost Jason Allen Miller, my only son, whom "God rest his Soul", I miss so very much.

I also take account of, my parents. My Dad Earl, who is more of a father to me than anyone can ever ask for, and my Mom who has endured my Sorrows beyond measure.

Thank you for everything.

To my Grandmother. Granny I love you. Thank you for your wisdom.

To Kim and Courtney, and Cary Miller, whom I will always carry close. And now Hailey, my Granddaughter, Courtney's very special gift. Welcome to the family to Andrew, Kimberly's husband, and to Ruby Valentine soon to be born. You will all be forever in my heart.

Also to Seana who has inspired so much.

To the part of my heart that keeps me real most of the time, I give to Lise. I don't deserve you, but I love you so very much and I am yours. I need you to know I am yours always.

To Lise's family as well, I love you and hope to be with you soon. I am trying, begging her even.

And now. Welcome to my "Book of Counted Sorrows".

By A. Tasman I

Sorrow of Losses

A merry heart maketh a cheerful countenance: but by sorrow of the
heart the spirit is broken.   Proverbs 15:13

We have all endured pain from loss of one kind or another. This section
is about losses endured and sorrow felt as a result.

Nothing Else Will Work

I've tried them all…
And none can take away the hurt,
Like the one that beckons me.
Hear now that oh so distant call.

Like no one else…
You take away this waking pain I feel.
It seems though when I need you most,
Someone from you my love they steal.

You wait so patiently…
This must be so very hard to do.
I'll keep the faith,
Grow tired of that, I now must surely do.

You give me strength…
And will to carry out all I do seek.
Though there still come times,
I feel so very ,very weak.

I get more than ever needed…
And just from holding on to you.
Your faith in me so strong, you see,
When I think of all for me you now have done, and do.

I feel so very wrong…
Yet I only do what's done you see?
For I love you more than words can say,
For what you have caused me now to be.

So wonder not my love…
This will be long after time is to us gone.
In a billion years you'll surely see,
Your love is all I need to keep me keeping on

This verse I write to you..
While miles away in ever pouring rain.
You bring warmth into my cold, and chilled, and weary soul.
You take away the burdens of life's never ending pains.

I need nothing now…
Not even touch of the precious flesh of you I find.
For when I think of only you
There comes this so needed peace of mind.

This Flower

You came to me freely,
And told me you loved me.
From that moment I have always known
Yes a chance had to happen,
That was not intended, but what a flower has bloomed
From this seed that was sewn.

Yes you know how to love me,
And you know how to taunt me,
And to make me to see things so true.
You're not like anybody,
I've ever met, that's for certain.
Yet I can't see living now without you.

Our souls seemed to reach out,
And to touch one another,
In a different, and so special way.
I never had dreamed,
That love could feel as it does now,
And for you to just know me, now I do pray.

For we sometimes put so much,
Between what is so important,
And that drops us a level or two.
It would be so damned easy,
For us to just let it all go.
I just thank God for the good sense to know now what I do.

So if I sound like I'm angry,
It's only that I am worried,
That someday I'll look up, and you will be gone
So…please ride these waves with me,
Till this ocean in my mind has stopped storming,
And is once again so peaceful, and calm .

I do not want another,
And I do need you so much,
To make this poor half, be once again whole.
So come to me now Baby,
Lets take this bad that now hurts us,
And let us once again touch our souls.

I Need For You To See

Don't know why it feels this way!
Don't even care you see?
For when we are loving like we do,
All other things just cease to be.

There's only you , in my whole world,
When you make love to me.
I feel so much a part of you,
And I know I'll always be.

You make me see a side of life,
That I have never known.
I thank the lord so high above,
For all you are, and all you've shown.

I also thank you too my love,
For being such a friend
I love you now, and always will.
I'm yours through thick, or thin.

The Perfect Girl

This is not just luck which you possess,
And still you cannot even see.
For the luckiest day of my life here,
Is when you first, did speak to me.

Now don't let it go my lady,
To your pretty head
Just because you are so gorgeous,
And really great in bed.

Don't think that I don't notice,
The little things you do.
I notice almost everything,
But you are only being you.

You are not so very perfect,
But only in your eyes.
For if I say you are not
My heart is surely telling lies.

So stop and think this evening,
While taking off your clothes.
This is a very special love,
And that's just the way it goes.

So, yes I will admit it,
I am quite lucky so it seems.
Just look at me I'm stuck for life
With the perfect girl of all my dreams.

For One So Young

Where have you gone?
Your presence sometimes fills my soul.
I must be graced by such a one
That warmed so many hearts once cold.

You've now moved along...
Your way was paved before your time.
Wish only I could be as strong
As was your noble peace of mind.

His emptiness now felt
Comes solely due to selfish pride.
Though tragedies cards to us were dealt
Heaven now is surely graced...this cannot be denied.

For one so young...
You made me see, where once so blind.
Through all the wrongs and rights now done
My purpose here you've surely helped me find.

I love you, precious son...
Though you have gone, you've taught me more it seems
Than any which since then has come.
I'll join you soon, but now must only be in dreams.

Suicidal Indulgences

Suicidal indulgences, entice in slumbered states...
Reminiscent of what was from lives gone past.
Yet happenstance does broaden, for whom with patience waits
To envelop once again, what has been forever cast.
Our fates are somewhat destined, but still we have a choice.
We can get it right this time, or return to try again.
To love you now with all I have, so cries my inner voice.
Lest we shall miss out on love, like none have ever seen.
So if you think I'm laying guilt on you...it's only cause I am.
You are much more than games you play to pass the time.
For if I didn't really care for you, I wouldn't give a damn.
I'd release these memories of you I still find.
You don't know I'm sure, or you would never let me feel this pain.
It makes me want to die, when I still wake alone.
The tears inside my heart still fall...hard as a summer rain.
Longing for you someday, to bring your love back home.

Reach Deep!

Reach deep...pull up the strength you so much need.
You've lost so much; yes this is oh so very true.
Then would be felt by everyone indeed
If came the loss of you.

It may never really be as for so long we all did dream
Still now you must reach deep to rise above it all.
For purpose here is not always as we'd have it seem
So reach deep to hear and heed of loved ones call.

You know not my heart or pain inside for you I feel...
For I now reach deep that I may hold back the flood of tears.
From cards of life so dealt to us, now look to what is real.
Know that we all hide pains...and sorrowing of fears.

Reach deep...as many times I have had to do
But know your worth is so much more to those you love.
Reach deep and draw from the depths of courage held inside of you
Reach deep...find purpose here and move to rise above.

Reach deep... and know that for you and yours I'm here.
So ask of me what you shall need and it shall be
For it's taken so very long for me to finally become aware
But now my eyes have opened wide and so much I see.
Reach deep...

That Bed Of Roses

It's been so very long since I went away and left you all alone
But let me tell you this while it's still on my mind.
There never passes any day, though I'm not with you any more
I don't find thoughts of you so far another world another time

I knew that loss we shared would drive the wedge too deep.
Maybe that's why I can't stop this suicide I chase today.
You might not know the pain I do feel so deeply that I now keep
Because I never got to say goodbye before I went away.

I may not be the one you love maybe you never really did.
I know that bed of roses had too many thorns you see.
But I'd die a happy man right now if this pain so long I hid
Will let me tell you that I love you before you say goodbye to me

Till The Stars Fall

Well now, you tell me you will love me
Till the stars fall from the sky
Well, don't talk no more, just let me see
Come on, Baby now and show me why
That you are different than all of the rest
Come on I'm giving you the chance to show
This is so easy now…will you fail the test
like so many others would…that I do know?
I put my heart gently into your hands…
Now what will you do to let me see?
Can I have faith in you and keep my plans
Or should I go ahead and set you free?
Was it all a game to pass the time
Or do you really think that we can do it?
Or was all that you claimed just another line?
Because if that's the case then screw it.
I'm so real about what I say to you,
And if you let it slip now so far away.
Don't say it's just because you never knew
Cause you still have the chanceif ou come back today.
So, don't let go unless you know for sure
Because my love will never let you down
This is a promise…now can you endure?
If not then there's no sense in hangin around.
So only tell me that you love me
If you are sure now you want what's real.
Because if that's not it then let me be
I have enough pain already that I can feel

I want you if you want to love me back
But not if only when and where you choose
I'll let you go and never take you back
If it looks like a game I'm bound to lose.
If you can look me in the eyes
And say you're here though all of it,
To where I will know
Then take off your shoes,
Sit down now, come to stay
Because my love for you will only grow
And if indeed you're going to love me
Till all the stars fall from the sky then put your hand in mine
and you Will see
That I am the one…yes I am the guy,
That will love you, yes till time does end
And never will there be
Another with you my love I'd like my life to spend
It's so much better than it's been with any other.
I know I've got good love for only you
Just say the word now and you'll see

My Special One

I love a girl who talks with angels,
And I can feel it when they're here.
And though she knows she's special sometimes,
She doesn't like what else is near.
When she is calling on her angels
Those voices come that do deceive
So when she ignores the voices in there
She hurts the ones that in her believe
But she's my special one still.
No matter what will happen or who's love she'll kill.
She's my special one and that always she'll be.
Because I'm the special one and that always her heart I see
Yes, she's my special one.
And I've seen all the others turn away
From the pain inflicted from her wrath
But I know she's only making sure
That's what keeps me in her path
And if I stay long enough
The smoke will clear and it will die down
And she'll talk again to those angels
And love me more for staying round.
And she's my special one still.
No matter what pain has been inflicted,
Or how much love has been killed
She's my special one and yes,
That always she'll be
For I'm that someone whose special enough
To inside that special heart see,
Yes, she's my special one.
We've been all we can be to each other
And way beyond all we can see
We can feel these forces driving

Where nobody else can be
And so if one of us goes off
And reaches too close too the sun
That's when we reach for one another<s
Love then back to the other run
And she>s my special one.
No matter if you can or cannot see.
Yes, she's my special one
And always in my heart her love will be,
Yes, she's my special one.
So, I'll let her talk to angels
Cause inside my heart I know
There is no body whose as special
And my love for won't go.
And I'll stay with her and to me
She can never be too wrong.
Cause she is my very special one
And my love for her is strong.
And you're my special one
And yes you know who you are.
Yes, you're my special one
And will be forever more.
And you're my special one
And this will always stay the same
And she's my special one
And soon she'll share with me my name
Cause she's my special one.

Her Love Belongs To Me

So she says you cannot hurt her, as you watch her slowly crumble
And you know the pain inside her is cause she can't let it show.
She'll say to you, she don't care, as she walks away in anger
But she's fighting back the tears, for fear your love will someday go
And you try so hard to tell her that you will not ever leave her
And to share the pain she's feeling, so that both of you can see
That the love you chose together, you gave freely to each other
Is a love that's like no other, or again will ever be.
And you feel the pain may kill you, cause you love her oh so deeply.
Yet you still fight to keep together, before you lose all self control
And break you down so low you can't see, to put back your life together.
Because you thought somehow together is how you would always be
And as she crashes from the hurting of the miles she's put between you
Hoping that she hasn't seen you, for something less than what you are
Cause inside she needs so badly for you once again to hold her
And let you know how much you love her, that pain don't matter anymore.
And though she went and left you lonely without nobody there to love you
She knew that she'd still be the only one, nobody else will do.
And as you hold her now so gently, and you feel your love inside her
And you know there is nobody who can love her quite like you
Now though your heart is oh so broken from the pain you are now feeling
It's still not bad as when your kneeling asking God for her return
And now once again you have her, were the pain and tears all worth it?
For the chance that you're now taking, for this to be that lesson learned?
And you know you felt the hurting from the pain as she was leaving
So I beg you, God, to let her finally this time to be mine.
And I love this one so special that no matter how she's hurt me
I know that I can't desert her now. No this will never be fine

So for now for me to hold her and know it is not her really
It's what someone else has taught her and still she's trying hard to see
And I love this one so special, so that no matter how it's hurt me
I know that I can't desert her now, because her love belongs to me.

Soothed By Loving Touch

The days now come so easily,
Because of truth which I now see.
An easiness I've searched for, for so very long.
Now binds our souls, makes our love so strong.

There still are doubts, but not so much,
That are not soothed by loving touch.
So as our souls do still entwine.
Brings easiness, love so divine.

Don't let us lose, not further fate.
That ever let us feel first hate.
Which make these days come easily,
So love is all someday we'll see.

Sweet Smelling Ointment

I wake to the smell of sweet almond smelling ointment
But not near soon enough. No this time it is too late
I meant only to doze for the briefest of moments.
But the hours have past and now I've found my fate.

The scent oh so sweet caused me to carelessly go
To places before not known, even in dreams
And once I woke the realization to know
That this was the end of my worldly schemes.

As I reached for the one I thought was my brother
And likewise to the girl who to me gave such love
And had vowed so many times, "No there is no other"
Even swore this so solemn to the Gods up above.

I know now the plans laid, ran so very deeply
I now hope for their pleasures each other to share
They must never have dreamed after lifes final sleeping
Comes with death realization and all absence of care.

Now I wait till the time when their waking eludes them
Then I'll carry out my plan, so they'll both surely see
The smell of the same ointment first her and then to him
And the time it will come back together we'll be.

I can just see the looks on their pitiful faces
As they finally know what did really transpire
Instead of just my life, to exchange brief embraces
Now to this world has caused all three to retire.

Others Never Feel

I sit and wonder where you are
And feel such mixed emotion
My world to you is only love
And all of my devotion
And once we had so very much
That others never feel
I want again to kiss your lips
And know our love is real.
You tell me that you love me
Yet you break my heart
I cannot tell you what it does
To be so far apart.
You made me see a side of love
Before I'd never known
By making things seem Beautiful
With each day our love had grown
I hope someday again you'll be my
Girl like once before
If not then I will never love
Not now or ever more.

Wicked Web

Oh what a wicked web we've wove.
From your mind all sanity they've drove.
For the laughs due to those not so strong.
To endure mind games, but not for long.
Now the tide it has turned, oh yes indeed.
Where before they all failed now they do succeed.
Now you see them through the slots in the door.
Rubber walls shall you know forever and more.
For you dabbled too deeply into their game.
And ended up with recognition, but surely not fame.
For soon they will forget all about you.
So those things that were stronger by far than were you.
Have now put you beyond the point of return.
And by selling out to them, yes in hell you must burn.
And it's too bad now, yes you've sealed your fate.
When you denied your own maker then you were too late
What a wicked web you've wove it's so true.
If you could do it again tell me, what would you do?

Peace Someday

I cannot seem to find the words
To make my feelings known not heard.
So you will maybe feel my heart
To understand what's me.
I never have meant nobody harm
From things I've said or done.
I think that hurt to me is all
I've ever wished to see.

I lost the one who meant to me
The hopes of ever being free.
And now to suffer needlessly
Comes from so deep inside.
I love you so, I hope you know.
And want your love for me to grow.
But seem so pushed away instead
So I run elsewhere to hide.

Confusion of what's now been done.
The many lost and few I've won.
Are battles I must deal with now
To hope for peace someday.
I know what's right, and what is wrong.
And hope this time there comes along,
A chance for me to find and use
The dues that I must pay.

I have so little left in me.
It's even hard for me to see,
A ray of light left for my grasp,
To pull me back from here.
So try to understand things I feel.
Inside of me it's very real.
And all I want is to be a part
Of those I hold so dear.

You re Not Running Me

I don't know what it is you think but check you're not running me
I've worked way too hard to be what now I choose to be
And you have no right to tell me where or how to live
I'll go where I want, do what I want and give if I wish to give
You say respect, and sometimes I wonder if you can spell the word
Because what is shown to me, is not what my ears have heard
You say so much but I think you talk to just look good
But what you say seems different than yuur deeds from where I stood
So now get right or be sure to be just left someday alone
Not knowing what is true, or lies, or erased tape, or etched in stone
My heart is pure, and I'll stand, and die if you need to be for you
Now look me in the eyes my friend and say the same is true
So don't talk that drag unless the walk is with it now as well
Because to cheat your love above all else will send you into hell
And if you can live by what you know to be the only way
I'll stand by you my friend until that final dying day

Son

How many times must I do this
And how many times before
Have I been here another time
I know I have I'm sure
We go through scenes, so acted out
As if they were rehearsed
When will the cost for all the pain
Be finally reimbursed
We travel on so many planes
When we finally get it right
I hope I'll be there with you soon
Just like some special nights
I feel your presence warming mine
As celestially we play
Not thinking of the pain I felt
Or the loss on that sad day
And it still brings tears into my eyes
To think I have to wait
To once again be with you, Son
And no longer self to hate
I miss you so and it's so hard
For me sometimes to see
That to end the pain so often felt
Is not how you'd have me be
So I'll go on through life on earth
Till together again we come
Pushing the people from my world
That have made my heart so numb
I promise you, my son, I'll be
With you again one day
So wait for dad and be good, Son
Till I can finally come your way

It s Time To Go

We had a lot of fun, and I fell into you
It was sort of like breathing just something I had to do
It seemed so good I couldn't quit and just let myself go
And it was more than you must see or ever will you know
I let you right on in and how I trusted your word
And that turned out to be just something somewhere you heard
For when I was down, you let me see just what to you was real
And didn't even seem to care who hurt or how I would feel
And then you lied and said so what and I still couldn't see
That if I kept on loving you you'd take all that there was left of me
And now you're playing one last game to see if you can have the last say
Well you can have it all, my Dear, cause I've paid out all the pain I'll pay
And maybe someday down the road if our paths happen to cross
You'll see if you would have really been right then now you'd not feel loss
But you're too proud and think you're too smart for anyone to see
Well you could be proud and if you were real you'd still be here with me
And now I know though I am sad from the loss of what I thought we had
That it's better if we just take separate paths lest once again it all goes bad
For you think I must be blind, as well as stupid, well it's time you know
I'm not now, nor have I ever been and that is Why it's really Time to go
You act as if you're doing me a favor to share what you think you can
Well check this out, I want one that's real so I'll hang tough not give a damn
Don't do me any favors with your so called promises that are really lies
Enough is enough and you're way too much to let you put tears in my eyes
And you've broke my heart so bad this time, I'll not soon let any other in
And nobody can ever take me to the places that we have been
But some of those places now I see are places I don't care to know
So this is why if you need a clue that Baby it is time to go

Straight Deceived

You can play with ones emotions for just so long
Before comes the time to pay and it it's not right
Comes time for you to see that it was wrong
So now I say so long instead of fight
But don't think it wasn't really, my friend
I felt every bit of pain and what a thrill
And what could or could not have been
Like a cold hard burst of rain oh what a chill
And to know I actually believed the lies
And all the while I was straight deceived
Yet I was still the one that tried
Now the one that is so bereaved
And you were so much less than nice, yes not to kind
I should have been well prepared to see
And still it's hard to see beyond my mind
With out what's really real to only me
Then there's a chance my heart by now
Would have had time to mend I can't deny
And I would have seen when as well as how
The masters men have served what's your reply

They're Watching

I know that they're still watching me
And someday I'll end this game
But every time I turn to see
They seem to fade away
I know they're, there and oh so real
I have seen them with my eyes
They come at night when others sleep
So good is their disguise
I don't know who for sure they are
And so I trust no one
I'll track them down however far
With the rising of the sun
But oh so careful must I be
When dark falls on this land
And why so badly they want me
I do not understand
So sleep eludes me due to fears
They changed the one I loved
I had no choice, now only tears
And I sent her up above
They took her mind and took control
Then she was one of them
And though I sinned just God will know
She last was seen with him
Just one more line, just one more day
This time I'll get the edge
And they're the ones who then will pay
For the depths they've drove this wedge
That's not enough! It's been too long!
What's this! Are you one too?
Then it's time to kill again, be strong
What else is there to do

The Light

What is this voice that's calling me...
And telling me to come
A strange bright light is all I see
I know not where it's from
I feel the strangest I have been
Like nothing I have known
Yet I see more than ever seen
From where comes this light that's shown?
It's growing brighter drawing near
I can't seem to get away
The wind so loud I cannot hear
Still it causes no dismay
I should be fearful of this thing
But my mind no longer cares
Of any harm that it may bring
Or that I should be aware
Oh now I know what last recalled
When I did start to doze
The snowflakes through the window saw
Just right before I froze
So now I know what light is this
That draws me like a flame
And look all those that I've so missed
But I can't recall their names
But I know of love we once so shared
As we walked upon the earth
And now I know to not be scared
Of this so called second birth
But wait the light is fading back
And so quickly I descend
And I feel your breath where mine did lack
And I thought you were my friend

Penguin Dreams

I was sitting here reading of those penguin dreams
But my mind kept on drifting to other strange things
Like how fucked up it is I am here and you're there
And how it so seemed you had just ceased to care
I think back to the days when all things were so fine
And wishing right now you were once again mine
I think that sometimes this is never to end
And then you send a letter that makes me so spin
But you always seem somehow to get back on the right track
And one I relax you break my balls then my back
So check this out, Baby, when next you pick up a pen
You'd just better be careful of the mood you are in
Cause if you think for a minute when my time here is done
And it will be as before, when you try to fly to the sun
I'll tell you now, honey, sorry I have to be blunt
If you ever think about speed, I will kill you, you butt

Running From Destiny

Not quite long as it does seem
Came the time to end all dreams
That's when the wrath of all my schemes
Crashed down upon me

I am still young, this may be true
But I've lost so much, now I've lost you
No matter what I seem to do
You still just can't see

Now I will keep to what I trust
Forgetting all that hurts so much
The things we lost for one more rush
Which now can not be

And I will run, running from destiny
Chasing the dreams hoping to find
Those things that are meant to be
Yes I will run...run till that day
I find myself and know the truth
Is down the path life laid

It's been so long since I once knew
Together things which we did do
The hopes and dreams we did pursue the way it was

And things got tough and we let go
To love, to dreams and we both know
The time when love did cease to grow as since it has
But I hold on to dreams of you
In all I feel and all I do
I hold the love so close we knew
For what is does

And yet I run, running from destiny
Fighting the past the things I lost
That mean so much to me
I'll run away until the day
The truth inside so long denied
Shows me the proper way

Five years have come and gone since then
A long five years it's truly been
And yet it truly seems a sin
It had to end

II
Inflicted Sorrows

Is it nothing to you, all ye that pass by? Behold, and see if there be any sorrow like unto my sorrow, which is done unto me, wherewith the Lord hath afflicted me in the day of his fierce anger. Lamentations 1:12

Paranoid Dreams

I know they're watching, every day
I can feel it through all things I do
But when I look, they run away
You think me daft…but it's so true

They even watch me as I sleep…
For they wake me staring in the night
I see their eyes in shadows deep
They vanish when does come the light.

I know they will not let me be…
So I fight off sleep by every means
I'll catch one someday…watch and see
To end this wrath of paranoid dreams.

Don't let them catch you sleeping deep
They'll take your sanity away
So stay alert your mind to keep
Be not the next that has to pay.

The Fear That Comes

My days are so much longer,
Than for others, can't you see?
For I fear the sleep that comes,
Moreover, all the things it brings to me.

It takes me many places,
Which I don't really care to go.
It makes me see a side of life,
I'd rather not have to know.

It wakes me in confusion,
Of what is really real.
So if I'm sometimes different,
Its because I don't know how I'm to feel.

I don't know who I'm supposed to be,
From one day, to the next.
So, do not try to analyze,
What you could not yourself accept.

Just know I mean no harm to you,
Or anyone you see!
For I'm not sure whom I'll be next,
Or, who is really even me.

To Kimberly
You'll Be A Winner

You are a step above the others,
And you know this deep inside
Yes, it does show in how you do,
When at your best.
There's only you, and not another.
This could never be denied,
That can rise up to meet the challenge of this test.
You make me proud to be your friend,
For this is very rare indeed.
Most other fathers could not deal with what I do.
Just know I'll stand by until the end
Let not any one, or thing impede.
For none, wherever could dispel my love for you.
So go into this battle bold…
And hold your head up high
Know you're a winner…by the feeling in your heart.
Do not give up, keep what's been told
But above all else, know why.
You'll be a winner in whatever you impart.

Sweetness Lingers

The need comes to me... as now I lie asleep
This desire to taste so of your love so bitter it is...for to seem so sweet.

How can this feeling be... that tortures me so in my dreams?
Yes! So desperately fulfilling now yet to awaken oh so cold it seems

Why must again this curse be mine... to torment so, yet to please again?
Is this forever how it shall be... or for all times has always been?

Or if forever it must be, or only for a speck of time...
That we may share this love you see it's sweetness lingers in my mind.

It's Up To You

I feel the pain from sorrow because now I am so oppressed, you know.
Due, to the past mistakes I made in haste, I could not see!
I let them have their way with me, right from the start, I lost heart!
Now I feel the shame of how being so ridiculed can be.
I beg you now to hear these words of newfound wisdom, which I speak
And hope you heed and put up your guard and not feel the sting
That paralyzed so many good I have known that now their lives so waste
and only empty walls hear their tales of woe for too late they sing
For tis better yet by far to stand your ground when right you are and stick
to what is good, don't bend to weakness, friend!
It's easy to get weak if you listen to the words they speak
Do not push down their lies, but hear your own righteous cries to the end
For you can never truly face anybody else if you can't really face yourself
and how can you if you've let them win this war
For the war it will go on even if a battle they may have won
Know it's so much more now that you are fighting for
Yes, counted sorrows they may be and far too much to want to count and
wisdom brings on oh so very many more
But it's better to go down and frown in tears from their lies than to just lie
down and let them treat you like their whore
For they say it's what is right, to give in not fight you see and they will use
you till you are surely spent
And in your place they'll cost somebody else and still put you away in a
place where you by now have already went
Don't let their lies confuse your will my friend, you must see!
And inside you must know what you will do
For when you picked the cards up off the table that was it and now it's up
to no one else, oh not it's up to you!

Those You Love, They Steal

So…you wish to talk about right, and fair, and just, okay, I see.

Then let's start out with this what's not right and what shouldn't be.

Then you tell me if you still feel the same about the lies they tell and what's really real

About what is said that real should be though the lives of those you love, they steal

To put someone upon a shelf for needless pain because they chose to use and not refrain

Well, too late now, you see, my friend, the past is gone, but you still can break the chains

These pigs we put in charge…well, I say we, but how exactly they got there though I can't see.

They've told such lies, while looking in our eyes, and have pretended all along what's right to be.

I've lost so much to people of power that have now forgot our names…it's true.

Just more statistics to chalk up to them to raise the ranks, just look at all they do

They sting you so deep with their lies, and somehow hypnotize you to their side.

They convince you that their lies are true and now you too agree to things so long denied.

Look deep but don't look at their face lest you shall help them to enslave the human race.

You can't expect to ever win you see, if you turn away, become the prey, the chased.

So go tell someone else to just give up abandon what is the truth with little or no fight

But know inside you are who's weak and will not speak…For those you know are right.

If Count I Must

If I counted all my sorrows
Since the day my life began
Put them next to all the smiles
I know I'd still never understand
For the sorrows seem so many more
It's like I am just doomed
So when they come these days it's like…
They've always been presumed.
I can't remember happiness
Like the times we shared, you see
Or pains I felt that were as great
As the day when you left me
So if count I must, I hope to count
All the sorrows right away
So all the smiles I shared with you
Will be with me my last days.

As You Are

Close your eyes now…come and take my hand
We will drift among the stars
Or anyplace you choose is fine
Just come now as you are.

I'll take you where you want to go
Or we can stay right here
It doesn't really matter though
So long as you are near.

Just come with me and you will know
No better can it be
Than times so spent no matter where
As long as you're with me!

I Come To You

Come take my hand…
But only if you are sure
I'll make you understand
My thoughts and purpose is only pure.

And yes! I'll be your strength
And you will see the love I feel
To know I'll go to whatever length
To make you know my love is real.

The choice is yours to take…
Know only this, I will not let you down
And your feelings I won't forsake
And for always my love will be around.

So you decide…
I come to you with all my heart
Love will not be denied
If so you choose to let it start!

Our Counted Sorrows

Quit running now from what is only meant to be…
For one day you must surely face what's real
Stop turning away seeing what only you now want to see,
As well as killing pain to feel what only you will feel.

Someday you may awake when it is much too late…
And I will be far away though I did not choose this road
You have but now to turn away and I will not intervene your fate
But of you likewise, just one word now I'll gladly carry your whole load.

I've loved you for so long and yes I never should have let you go…
Still it's not right for you to kick me when so hard I now have fell
For you also have felt the vastness of our love, and you surely know
the lengths I'd go to have you in my arms and end this hurting hell.

Come now to me and stop what games you play to only pass the time…
for your games are scars you are inflicting now upon your soul
What has been so bought shall be sold also through your mind,
You know your karmic jots and titles shall someday al unfold.

OUR Counted Sorrows now exceeded more than surely meant to reach
So only we can cleanse the wounds for love of one another now
For of your love again I ask and humbly also I do now beseech
That once again we get the chance to share our love somehow.

Legends Finally Meld

Another leaf falls from the tree…
Sun fades from one more day.
How many more days will there
Be of this debt I now must pay?

Only a blinking of an eye…
For the billion tears now cried.
How many times shall we deny
Or how many lives have died?

Yes, one more year has left behind…
More memories, now harder gained.
A year of wisdom for the mind,
Yet one more key obtained.

The secrets of this mystery…
Inside all souls now held.
Till truth be found and light we see
And all legends finally meld.

When Will The Sunshine Come

When will the sunshine come…
There's been so much rain for so long.
Where is it coming from…
A tinge of sorrow in every song?

When will the sunshine come…
So little gained yet so much now lost
Or that's the way it is for some…
So little bought for so high a cost?

When will the sunshine come…
So close yet oh so far away.
What will life now become…
Since smiles came back with you today?

When will the sunshine come…
Are we meant to love eternally
Will this finally be the one…
That we were looking hard to see?

When will the sunshine come?

Waiting For The Sun

I cannot say in words what now I'd really like to say…
And just one day could never even be enough, you see
I'm falling more in love with you with every passing day…
And love with you is more I know than I ever dreamed could be
You've been there now so many times, I owe so much to you…
And I thank the Lord for sending such an angel at this time.
You go with me both night and day no matter what I do
And no matter what may happen I know I'm always in your mind
Once we get past the awkwardness, I know such love will bloom
Like a flower waiting for the sun to finally unfold.
I'm finding places in my heart where till now was never room
And looking forward so to times when in my arms you I will hold.

Such Sweet Remorse

My sleep is restless once again
I reach for you so helplessly
How many nights now has it been
How many more like this will be?

I chase you through my dreams in haste
A hope to grasp for in the night
To wake alone is such a waste
When love like this is oh so right.

Convicted by this soulful force
No sorrow more, so soon shall be.
For all now paid such sweet remorse
When I wake with you next to me.

Return

Frustration overcomes...
From efforts given so in vain
Till comes time when I must refrain
Or else let loose that one

Forever now subdued...
To keep such fury from their lives
But oh so futile are their tries
When once more freedoms been renewed.

Victorious now...
You have won the battle not the war
When I return you'll know what for
And I will slowly show you how.

Such solemn lies...
You've told to cover what is right
But I have not yet
Shown my might
But you'll know when all your now dies.

Suppress This Suffering

Untimely situations do so refract my fate…
However I refuse to veer from my love for you.
Knowing that my chance to progress may now dissipate
This urgent energy propels my soul through all I do.

Driven by primeval forces, which I can't restrain…
These vicious acts inflicted now, does such sorrow so instill
Yet my heart belongs to only you, no matter how much pain
I've tried but cannot suppress this suffering, I so wish I could kill.

You're the solution for which I've searched for oh so very long…
My karmic chance to give back what for so long I did repel
So give to me the chance to love you, know it isn't wrong
For without you in my world you see, I'm living in such hell

When first we touched, inside myself, I felt I always knew…
Of love misplaced, so long ago, to start us on this trail
Knowing if you would take my love, as also I'll take you
Then we will reach that highest plane together without fail.

Captive Dreams

I can almost taste your lips on mine
As we merge as one this night.
This love we share is more than fine
No regrets are had when it's this right.

I can feel the current flow throughout
Our passions caught in time it seems.
Knowing this is what true loves about
Though only felt now in our captive dreams.

It won't be long till we can feel
The pleasures held back by this test
But if we do pass the worst that's real
Then forever we can share the best.

I know inside you're made for me
As I am so made just for you
So give yourself to love and see
Such perfect love you never knew.

Hold On

Hold on…hold on to what you know is true.
We have been so far so many miles
Hold on…through all that's asked of you
Through the joys, the pains, the tears, the smiles
Hold on!

Hold on…I've never loved like this before
You have my heart encompassed now
Hold on…and love and know what for
Don't try too hard for we know how!
Hold on!

Hold on…for ever we have needed this
And have denied so many times this love
Hold on…for to know what waits is to know bliss
And to become one inside…as well as far above.
Hold on!

Hold on…I will not ever let you go
Though we've been through all this before
Hold on…and we'll learn together what there is to know
And so move on now through that final door.
Hold on!

Once More Alone

Your smile it fades…
As now I wake once more alone.
Thoughts of you my mind evades,
Wishing so you were back home.

My eyes blink closed…
A tear rolls down my cheek
This sorrow my heart so well now knows,
Makes pain come when I hear you speak.

I push away all thought…
And rise once more to meet the day
With hope you…I will think of not
Lest till again I sleep…my heart must pay.

On The Line

We've put our lives on the line…for what?
To be ridiculed, locked up, turned out in the street
Well, that ain't right and I'll tell you now it sucks!
Its their bureaucratic asses we really need to beat

Treated like pigs, put in the back of their minds to sleep
Well it's time we now really fight a war that's for what's right
Not for land owned by those who don't want no pain to keep
But for illicit trade to put money in their pocket we so did fight

Well, the truth is known by all and yet we still can't see
That's not what our forefathers would have chose to do
To let them shrug it off and say that's just the way it has to be
Well, I'll tell you now, it's up to not only me, but it's up to you

So stand up, be heard, don't let them talk over your mind
Wrapping up in so much red tape what's inside your head
Or someday you'll wake up trapped by them, enslaved to find
Thinking, look at us now! I think we'd all be better off dead

The war they wage is to get us that know out of the way
Of the games they play where they do what now they are
Taking down more good me day by miserable day
Well, don't you think this time it's gone a bit too far?

Trail Of Sorrow

The trail of sorrow...
So long it seems.
But still we borrow
To meet our dreams.

The pain we know...
Shall ease some day.
But cannot go...
Till debt we pay.

The price is high...
To reach the top.
Don't stumble child...
Lest you should stop.

He'll take you through...
Those troubled times.
Have faiths the key...
To ease the mind.

Grace Redeemed

Such sacrifice for us have made
To put back light so scattered now
For a million years of debts not paid
By love and grace redeemed somehow

Oh child of mine with little faith
Let go of worldly snares that bind
And move on to a better pace
Where you won't have to look behind

It's but your choice to come or stay
But heed this warning, lest you die
It's time to choose, no time to play
Put trust in self not asking shy.

Karmic Wealth

The seconds pass away...
So slow it seems they take to fade
So long appears each day...
As waking hours I so evade.

Too long now so it seems...
Since last our love was taken in.
I only have you now in dreams...
My lack of sleep tells how it's been.

Come back and ease my pain...
We inflict such torture to ourselves
Let not our pride, this love disdain,
And rob us of its karmic wealth.

Too much has passed us by...
From times forgotten long ago
We run from destined love and cry
When it's what must be and this we know.

Don't run away again...
Let our souls be one, to move along
Let our love...now take us in
Knowing never love like ours was wrong!

Euphoric States

Entwined so long by circumstance…
My spirit searches to no avail
Is this to last eternally
Pursuing your love only to fail?
Then assuming what you pose as mine…
Eludes again to be mirage
The sorrows reign till back you are
Inflicting their heart sent barrage
Facetious acts do hit their mark…
My soul engulfed cries out again
For love abstruse as ours so is must deem
The worst of mortal sin
However when we both give in
To take the other by loves hand
Euphoric states so overtake
And in our souls we understand.

Look Alike Birds

You've lived so many lives it's true
And to time, you're no new hand
All the wrongs done in the universe
I'm so sure you understand
Like it may be true of wisdom dear
You have so much for sure
Beneath the rage that's housed atop
Beneath you are so pure.
Also you have such insight
To oh so very many things
It helps I'm sure, this little bird
With the warnings that it brings
Now I wouldn't want to change your mind
Because I know of your intent
The good to all you love I know
Is how your time is spent
But someone now and then you see
Seems to take you by surprise
By sending look alike birds to you
That tell you only lies
For I would never do you harm
And for sure where we're concerned
Because to lose your love will mean
That I am being burned
So check your bird more carefully
Next time he speaks of me
Cause if it's bad, it's not your bird
But an imposter don't you see.

III.
Sorrow Of Humility

And unto Adam he said, Because thou hast hearkened unto the voice of thy
wife, and hast eaten of the tree which I commanded then saying, Thou shalt
not eat of it: cursed is the ground for thy sake; in sorrow shalt thou eat of
it all the days of thy life.
Genesis 3:17

The days of our years are three score years and ten; and if by reason of
strength they be fourscore years, yet is their strength, labour and sorrow:
for it is soon cut off and we fly away. Psalms 90:10

Surely he hath borne our griefs, and carried our sorrows: yet we did
esteem him stricken, smitten of God and afflicted. Isaiah 53:4

I'm afflicted...she's addicted.

This Prey Pursued

What livid minds cannot conceive…
Where be all mortal thought concerned
That doors may open to these souls
Lest time shall leave them ever spurned

To grasp wistfully at fading hopes…
From lives forgotten in despair
So given to another's soul…
Without remorse your fate impair!

So blinded by love this intense…
Your universe seems so to elude
So venomous this love does seem
Yet still you yearn this prey pursued.

To merge as one your final goal
To move on lest ye shall rescind
To begin this peril one more time…
In hope this journey soon shall end.

Plastic Lover

There will never be another
That has so much power over me
Just me and my plastic lover
So much of my blood in you shall be.
You take me on such trips…
To places only we can go
Don't need no planes or ships
To reach heights only we will know
I need only you, my friend
Can't be replaced by no other
You're with me till the bitter end
I love you my plastic lover
But now I've met someone
That makes me feel things I've never felt
If I choose you then we're done
So now I must draw to cards I've dealt
So I must let you go now…
It was fun but now I see
There's one that cares much more now
Though it's hard I guess I'll set you free
And there will never be another
That taught me what now I have learned
But you my plastic lover…
From me all of her love you have now turned.

You Are The Meek!

What thoughts through troubled minds now pass...
Let not us judge, what not we know
From troubled past comes pain to thee...
But burns so deep it dares not show
You've put the wedge between your lies...
to cover what was never wrong.
Condemning those who's spirit dies...
To knock out the fight from those once strong
You raise yourself by circumstance
Intending that no one will see...
For those you cripple, with your lies of chance
Are the ones your nightmares soon shall be
For what does come, shall surely go...
And you'll find out, if you so play
With the lives of those you do not know...
To hell condemned someday you'll pay!
You say it's for the good of all...
I ask you now, of whom you speak?
look into my eyes so you'll recall
When comes the day...you are the meek.

So Long Apart

Hello, we've been so long apart
O ask you now again…
But take your time do not return…
If you fear again to break a heart.

We both have had the time
To know if love is real…
Yes, I'm convinced it's for your love
I search so in my dreams to feel

Come back but on your own
My door is open to only you
Come if you dare to know the truth
My love belongs to you alone.

For now the past must matter not
Except that love was always ours
Since God set the souls to find their way
And created with his love the starts

Come back…we've been so long apart.

Let Go

Let go...relax and set the world aside
Know not only of the toils you can do for them
Let go of those who have you so oft denied

Your time at hand here is but so brief
Let go...let go, if it so hinders you
Let go, let not such annoyances cause you grief

Let go...don't bend to whims which mean only to test
You know your limits so far do theirs surpass
Let go, your very worst vastly exceeds their best.

Rise above these earthly snares you've come to know
Let go... know why are these things now you must do
Let go of all that makes your journey slow, let go.

Tear Down These Walls

These walls between us anger me…
I call to you in dreams at night.
In waking hours such agony
Instinctually comes the urge to fight.

To protect you from a world so wild…
To hold you safely at my side
This circumstance has now love beguiled
And passions pleasures too denied.

Release me now, my place to take…
You in my arms where you belong
With all urgency such love we'll make
No longer will life seem so wrong.

Tear down these walls and set us free
To love, like love was meant to feel
Just me with you and you with me
More than you dreamed almost surreal.

IV.
Sorrow Of Mind

And among these nations shalt thou find no ease, neither shall the sole of thy foot have rest: but the Lord shall give thee there a trembling heart and failing of eyes and sorrow of mind.
Deut. 28:65
The sorrows of death encompassed me and the floods of ungodly men made me afraid. Psalm 18:4

Selfless Hell

So often we don't take the time…
So needed to atone intents.
Neglect of soul is more a crime
Of which there's little recompense.

Your deeds irrelevant when convictions pent
As purpose must be not of self
For that which from the heart is sent
Are those more oft whence we should delve

I can't deny this love so great
You denote more than mere words can say
Return now lest this disintegrate
For I have waged all I will pay.

I have chased you since time first began
And came so close but again have fell
Still you pursuing time and again
To live once more in selfless hell.

Intensity

Intensity…takes from what I do
To pull me toward you once again
Intensity…from love for only
You make life erstwhile seem such a sin
Intensity…from whence passion shared
Had made the rest seem so passe
Indeed intensity like never dared
Had made this game too hard to play
Intensity…keeps my faith confused
Not knowing what be my next step
Intensity…of rage from feeling used
Where secrets known should still be kept.

Essence

Essence of my love for you…
So present with each breath I take
I feel you in all things I do,
Was loving you my worst mistake?

Essence of you still lingers strong…
No matter what I think or feel
My choice to love you has turned so wrong
For now to love you would be to steal.

Essence of right surrounds my mind…
I know you're living such a lie
Still I can't taint these things I find
Nor can your love I now deny.

Essence of me so wants you here…
To feel what both know is so good.
Essence of you to me brings such fear
Like none before have or ever could.

Whatever Price

Seek that now which will your journey guide
Do not impede your search for light
Be aware of thought for thoughts can't hide…
From those whom have attained the right.

Go on your way to where you feel
But always know your hearts intent.
Put forth what's known as right and real
Only love and light from self be sent.

As you prepare to journey on
Be aware of which path you so choose
For one wrong choice, what's gained is gone
Once more in debt to pay your dues.

We have learned so much by crossing paths
Found limits never since obtained
Felt much both of love as well as wrath
Still love this deep shall be sustained

If again our paths shall chance to touch
And I can help you on your way
Know loving you to me…means oh so much
Worth whatever price that I must pay.

For THE CAUSE
To My Brothers AT ARMS

Time Draws Near

So...you don't like all the waves I make?
So whatLet me tell you this then...
But listen good our daughters and also our sons
Don't get weak in the middle or their threats your will break
For to submit to them is sure the worst of all the sins you'll by then done
So get right...or get left, lie down for good
And get out of the way
Or stand up...the way you should,
Don't bow down to their games they with you play
You live but once as this one, here and now...
This is so true nothing after is guaranteed
So for those of our blood that follow our lead, is what now
To do and try our best to succeed
It will get allot worse before it all comes to a head,
and the forces will be held no longer at bay
So think long and hard my child when you choose the side
where you'll stand on from this day
Time draws near for the people again
to become one to once again unite
To overthrow this evil
that has now so long here been and again set things right.

All Time To Come

What joyous feeling... to me you bring
When you but share your heart.

You make me aware... of everything
When you impart.

So do not cry... for that we've lost
We have all time to come.

When we are one... no more the cost
To us...but still for some.

As Once Had Been

I chase you through the skies
Over the mountain tops, among the stars
I do wonder why so slow now flies…
The time that we must remain apart.

What took you from me…I don't know!
But know so the sorrows now I feel
I know pain so inside yet still does grow
Reminding me of our love so real

I cry out in dreams for your return
But wake to only empty air.
Where so intense I felt your love…
Your lips, your touch, your passion rare.

If life was but to never feel just in our dreams
I know I'd wake not…for fear again
I know nothing is as sometimes it seems
But would wish for you as once had been.

Distant Battles

This incessant dispensation so seduces me
And convening are our souls as now we sleep
Our destiny is hanging, like so many clouds you see...
Awaiting our precipitation but for now we both must weep.

Though this incubus engulfs our very entities
As we seek so one another throughout the night
We both understand with such age old familiarity...
That this our quest to love as one is truly right.

We have eluded one another since before all time
Scared so of that final peace which now we seek
Where before to do what now we must would be a crime...
We share deepest secrets in our souls yet need not even speak.

Although we've waited through the ages how slow time now does pass
until together once again as planned for oh so very long
This love of ours shall surely all the rest combined surpass...
For distant battles waged through time have made us strong.

Mystical Desires

Gripping illusions…
So fill my troubles mind
While thought should be somewhere afar
Mystical desires of only you I find.

Gnashing emotions…
Tear at my suffering soul
This part of me is your alone
So far you are away inside I seem so much less whole.

Foolish pride…
I feel such shame from trusting lies
This weakness of myself defiles my heart
From so deep hear my souls sorrowed cries

Eternal love…
Belongs to you and I am so much afraid
This pain I feel from loss of you
Not much more can I bear what's been paid

Serendipitous Slumber

Amid serendipitous slumber I come to you again
First meeting…long since now past
Still good luck I feel from all we do…
And hope unconsciously love may still ask.

Mesozoic moonbeams that bind our souls…
As gods once bound with love and light
Cast off and hidden were our goals
By Brahma's will from sin of sight.

Condemned as mortals as we are now
The record cloaked from conscious mind
Though in my sleep returns somehow
Are flashes of love stole I find.

We fight this force which draws us in…
Because confusion has so been instilled
From others sin once gods now men…
Has made us wait because it's willed.

God's Door

Wicked is the mind of man...
Made so by Brahma long before
When soul is met we understand
And search again to find God's door.

For though we're here, but a short time
And so many lessons we need atone
Seek help through that inside you'll find
You never were at all alone.

It's up to you to get it right
How many times till you can see
That here as man is a mere plight
To get back where you use to be.

So set things straight with truth and love
And let all not needed pass
Go back where you once were above
Which to our souls will come at last.

Desolation Road

This desolation road has so much my fate now twisted
Where once I'd known of only bad that I so chose to see
Yet so many lies now told has my soul so much now blistered
Still what's good will come I know, I hold this truth inside of me.

This desolation road also makes so feel its tortures
That are only to us tortures if we let them in our heart
For the loss of what we hold so dear is the gain sometime to others
If we know when desolation road did start.

So I'll travel on my journey now assured of where I'm going
For my desolation road is only desolate by my choice
Bigger things are now in store inside my heart I'm surely knowing
Because above that desolation road I've now heard solutions voice.

Dad

Elite in all you've ever done
Assured in all you'll do
Remembering most everyone
Large hearted you are too.
Humane beyond what most can be
As well as so concerned
Never looking not to see
No matter how the tide has turned
Exceptional as people go
Much more than I can say
Always there for us this we know
No matter when both night and day.

For Sissy & Corky

A Poem For You

I miss you oh so very much
I miss your smile, I miss your touch
I miss you more than you could know
I miss you where ever you may go
I miss your feet, your eyes, your hair
I even miss that look you wear
I miss you so and this is why
My eyes miss you and so they cry
I'd walk a million miles or more
To see you till my feet are sore
I miss you so and only hope
I see you before my misser is broke.

Courtney Marie

Things Somehow We Last

I don't blame you for being mad
I know I've let you down
By being oh so out of reach
When you've needed me around
It makes me sad inside my heart
To always have to know
That you are so upset at me
Because I couldn't watch you grow
Well I only hope it's not too late
To turn some things around
And find some things some how we lost
That really do need found
For if I do not feel you love me soon
I don't know how much I can take
Till I fall all to pieces, girl
And my heart does finally break.

Look At Me

Just look at me today...
But looking from your point of view
I know you cannot see...
The way I look at things this way
The things that I've so chose to do
That's just what makes me be me.

Just look at me today...
I've seen so much in little time
Yet still I am right here
Well, if you choose to dance you must also pay
I'm just glad now of peace of mind
And the end of this journey is so near.

Just look at me today
You shake your heads and wonder why
I am not more like you
Well, that's because their games I will not play
About the truth I won't be shy
So now look at what it is you do!

Too Much Too Soon

I still smell the lilac in the air
Above the light which shone below
I can see you but can't seem to feel
Your skin so smooth which seems so now to glow.

But look who's that you're tending to?
It looks just like…this can't be so
The tears now coming from your eyes
Cause me concern…yet still I have to go.

I'm fighting hard to come back home
To hold you in my arms again
I never thought I'd leave you all alone
Just one last time…then honest it can end.

I only want to kill the pain!
I'll be alright just…let me be
Too much too soon I'm gone away
My final fix I swear…you'll see!

This Utopian Mirage

I chanced to wander upon this utopian mirage
Where nothing was quite as it was so portrayed
My eyes were open wide but I couldn't really see.
These things I thought were once so real that my consciousness was swayed.

I decided that I would check it out despite all of the cries which warmed
me of deception and of what would surely be
Yet still it looked so good and I thought myself so wise that I went in with
eyes wide open and still I couldn't see.

What kind of wizard runs this place? I had often asked myself to make
things look so appealing when they're poison to us all
To partake of such a journey I felt would surely bring me wealth but no,
instead I am the one who now must hear the call.

I know so much of lies now lived and pain I've had to feel that just one
more lie in my life, surely my will you'll take
I only want to share my love and feel what things are real
This utopian mirage was just designed to make hearts break.

Once More Fulfilled

Cast out so long ago…
Like a bomb which bursts into the sky at night
We have scattered through the many years
Each one a vital piece of this once so bright light.

We chose our paths…
Lessons learned will restore us back in time
When obligation has been once more fulfilled
Shall also come unequaled peace of mind.

So turn inside and see…
Let go of burdens to find familiar long lost love
Cast out all hate…seek only wisdom of the truth
So once again all light can come back to shine above.

The Silent Sword

The time goes by exceeding what seems real
I wait for word but none arrives not good nor bad
Impending darkness grows deeper, the air is cold to feel
What once was fear, now turns to the only freedom to be had.

Where once I knew my plight with life and all it's bounds
now matters not what's done as much the thought or so it seems
The placid soul dwells deep inside to finally come around
When mortal warriors cry out in vain, to die for others schemes.

Yet this must truly be to fill the prophesies let out so long ago
To bring the healing round to souls from so many lives now past
To pay the debts we owe to self for things we no longer even know
Still must be paid in full if this life here is to be our last.

Take up the silent sword of truth that lives inside us all
To slay the liars and their lies before it becomes too late
Ask only of the one inside yourself who cast your light to call
To rise for good out of this plane and thus fulfill this mortal fate.

For All We Owe

What's been by once so long ago
Comes around again at last
Fulfilling likes with same again
From forgotten days so far now past.

We pay for all we owe in time
And likewise all owed to us is paid
Lest not the prophecy be fulfilled
Our mortality shall again be stayed.

No soul can now progress you see
Until all required has so been met
So be all now that you can be
Let not the deeds you've done forget.

Take graciously the tares you bear
And rise above this worldly plane
For above the rest you so belong
Go like the moth now to the flame.

When It All Comes Back

When it all comes back around
These prophetic tales will all hold true
Our purpose here though seem to us profound
In time will be revealed in what we choose to do

It all holds to one course
Though different parts are played out now so well
To escape this prison cell
And find ones true light source
For to be past all this here
Is to avoid eternal hell

Our prisons are so much inside
For anyone that chooses so can be completely free
For once what is this world has been totally denied
You can move on to be what you are truly meant to be.

Devoured By Their Lust

I feel their seeking minds
Pursuing as I wake in shadows deep
As well enclosing about my world so fast
To try to take my mind as now I drift to sleep.

I must not slumber now…
Just one last line allows me to be on my way
To flee these demons as they engage
My wit to retain…at least another day.

I know they're coming soon
But I will run and avoid their tortures still
So not my mind to surely lose
All those I feel are evil…I now must kill.

I surely first will die
Before I let my soul be devoured by their lust
To kill you…once thought my only friend
If overtaken now…then yes, I really must.

What Is This Hell

What is this place…
Have I so much in life to fear?
When it seems now as seconds pass
They surely feel more like a year.

Why must I stay…
If God is good then what is this hell?
Where lies are told, and so much lived,
And prosper…only those that lie so well.

Is it still sin… to seek your fate as swift you can?
When to end this life you must return,
Lest you've met your debit true to plan?

If we're to shine…
Then why can darkness around us so abound?
As we go one and reach new planes to find…
Those things we know need found.

Friends

It's times like these that make me see
That friends are ones that know
There's more to this than getting by
and once you see you'll grow
A lot of people just play games
And think that's all there is
But they're the ones who'll never see
or really know true bliss
When I can talk to anyone
the way I talk to you
And know that I am understood
then guess what? This will do.
There are no games and so much is felt
But no regrets are ever had
unless someone has hurt my friend
Because that makes me mad
Cause when I choose a friend, you see
I'll be a friend for good
and be there through both thick and thin
Because I feel I should
And you've been my friend since we first met
and not so long its been but any time or any thing
I'll be here for you, my friend.

Distant Thunder

What distant thunder now reveals as cries are heard…
Where so long were subdued
The pleas of those so long oppressed now once more
Shall finally be at last renewed.

The lives they take are sacrifice to alert those held at bay
Although not justified
Where otherwise the wrongs go on
So long their freedom now has been denied

Still those in power shout
"these acts are cruel"…yet torture their own people so
With lies of how it soon will be…
It's time I feel that all involved should truly know

They even use the name of God
To promote these actions and cover all their lies
Well, if my life too will help the world
Then let it be that I'm the very next that dies.

You Broke My Brain

I really thought I'd found someone
That much we deeper than the rest.
That you made me fall so much in love,
And your acting was the best.
But now I see that's all it was
Now that it's turned around.
And the shoe is on the other foot'
And it's stomped me to the ground.
And I won't lay the blame on you
For how this all did start.
But I at least am trying hard,
So that we do not part.
You must not think at all of me
Or you would not forget
How much I loved you from the start.
I have not stopped that yet.
I must be crazy just to do,
The things I do for us.
And you say you love me babe,
But hey are you sure it's not mere lust?
Please stop the stupid things you do
Before I go insane.
You've broke my heart and that's not all,
You've really broke my brain.
So now I beg you one more time,
To be what you've portrayed.
And get our love back where it was,
And where it should have stayed.

The Dream

I dreamed a dream the other day,
In which the world had ceased to move.
But I hung on, defied the Gods,
Because of integrity still to prove.

The dream went on, the world grew dark,
And life we know had ceased to be.
And then I finally realized it,
They'd even taken you from me.

I knew that if I could just wake.
Then all would be as was before.
And so I tried to go back there.
But somehow, someone had locked the door.

And then I stood before a throne,
A mighty king looked inside my soul.
I knew that if I faltered now,
Again I never could be whole.

I told this king of this great vision,
In which all time had seemed to cease.
But how without you there beside me
My soul could never find real peace.

He looked so sternly, and he finally breathed
A sigh before he spoke.
He said my courage defied all logic.
How never before such rules were ever broke.

As I felt him breathe life back in me.
I felt your head upon my chest.
I knew not death could even part us,
Cause I was worthy of this test.

This Place Of Dreams

There is a place I often visit,
And not too many more can go.
For money cannot buy admittance.
Nor can the fact of who you know.

This place I speak of is so empty,
Unless you come to meet me there.
Because so few are even welcome,
Only those for which I care.

I go there more now than I use to.
Because you are so far from me.
For this is where we still together,
Can feel the other, though not free.

And I know the pain that you are feeling.
For I feel so much inside me too.
But never think that you're alone
For I am always there with you.

And miles are only miles between us.
If in our hearts our love does stay.
Then we will live in dreams together,
Among stars where just we can play.

So if you feel as I am with you,
It's probably more than it does seem.
For nobody else can even reach me,
Where I meet you, inside my dreams.

I hope to see you there my lover.
So I can have you by my side.
And we can share that special feeling,
That now these walls have so denied.

Nobody else has ever captured,
Parts of my heart that you do hold.
And love I feel for you so deeply,
Is the best of love before untold.

More Than You Are

Well, you think that you are too tough...
Better think again, it's very lonely at the top
And when every one else really gets rough
You'll be all alone, no place to turn, ready to drop
Cause it's dog eat dog and only the strong...
To be sure, but you know all of that, I just forgot.
You've been playing this game so very long...
That you think the rules you can bend but guess again, NOT!
Now you stepped right out of your league...
And surely out of what's left now of your mind.
It must have been over stress or fatigue...
What were you expecting, or even thinking you'd find?
Where they now play, the game, they play for sure, for keeps...
No prisoners you see, too much is now at stake
For he who gets weak is he who in the end weeps...
And is the next example of whom they will make
So before you check in better check this out...
And know the odds before you start are small
That if you end up like what you think you're not so tall.
And all because you had to be more than you are...
Well don't be, because you want to impress me
I'll be impressed more now by very far
By showing how real you are
And how real you will be.

In Darkness Of The Night

Only those elite are chose to bid
For fools who'll never see
By powers hand all things are planned
But without the truth what really can it be.

We've set ourselves upon such shelves
At times when others sent out their cries
Only to win by the wage of sin before
This mortal body finally leaves this earth and dies.

How far must we go till we finally know
That we are all part of this eternal total light
Still until we changed all will be strange
As long as we still choose to live in darkness of the night.

Confusion So Abounds

Confusion so abounds...
Now faced with what to do
When all would be right in it's time...
Yet knowing now inside how much I'm still in love with you

I'm asked to choose...
By some who can see my trials
Where you say to me not yes or no
To choose wrong now you see my intent it so defiles

You test my will...
Yet to you it's not a test
You know no better of this I'm sure
But from me to you I always gave my very best

I never let it go
My pride wants so to let you be
But my heart is hanging to this hope
That some day soon you too will see

What Once You d Shown

The forces pulled us close…
The chance had come at last to see
What would we do given no odds
Look now what's come to be

A lot was thrown into the works…
Both what was real and things unknown
Now you are there and her I am
Showing you what once you'd shown

It's not too late for us you see…
If we just can let go
Once more to share what once was free
And share what we so well did know.

What Can t Be Bought

It hurts too bad…
To try to go on…day by day
When all that matters to me is gone…
Am I expected still to stay?

I had given up on love so long ago…
Then you appeared
And spoke to me of what was real
Convinced I'd cast off all once feared

You took from me…
What can't be bought or sold, you see
You stole my heart and made it hard
So much now none could ever make love be

It's less than cruel…
To do as now you've chose to do
For love that none have ever known
Was my gift
And it was only meant for you

Sending Only Love

I'm sending only love to you
In order that I may still see
The purpose here eludes me so
Why can't things go more happily?

What started out to pass the time
Became so much a lesson learned
For what…to pay for lives gone by?
Must we this life keep getting burned?

I love you with the best intent
I'd never want for you to cry
I'd rather alone my life be spent
Than to think you sad the day I die

Stop Throwing Rocks

Stop throwing rocks as me!
I cannot take another day
You say you really love me but still
Such awful games you play
Stop throwing rocks at me!
You hide behind a mask of lies
You say you do not see
Or even hear my deafening cries?
Stop throwing rocks at me!
My love for you has changed it all
How much longer will it be…
Till on your own rocks you will fall?
Stop throwing rocks at me!

This Is But A Dream

Where leads this path with all it's obstacles
Which we must overcome?
We've set out so many times before...
Yet can't quite recall our mission or where it's really from

We both know the truth...
Yet still find it hard to not seek the lies
There's so much more that we can see...
Where so many others have so far to go to realize.

You have helped me know that this bond we share
Is much deeper than most see
For we don't have to posses to love
That's what makes it unconditional and oh so free.

My friend you will remain
My love is yours to share beyond this worldly scene
We seem to touch where others can't
Because we know in the end this is but a dream.

This Path Together

We have traveled down this path together
Though we have still remained so very far apart
These roads they deep us intersecting
And you never wander from my heart

I remember that first meeting too so long ago...
That final day of May
The tears stopped coming from your eyes
Once I told you it would be okay.

I fell in love that instant...
I only wish I knew what now I know
So much would be so different
And you would never ever wish to go

As this path together crosses now
I still love you now like on that day
But I'm the one with all the tears
Every time you turn to walk away.

This Flower II

This time now spent,
To share my thought and dreams I feel
So little yet so much of me
All secrets held…to you I would reveal

You touch my heart with what you feel
Of life and what it holds
Let now happen that which you so will
And see what joy this flower we've grown unfolds.

For love is real and taken now
As such a special sign
From me to you I give my heart in hope
Your heart shall also now be mine.

You seek my love yet fear
To reach and take my hand
Still something brought you back to me
I'm hoping this is what for us was planned.

What Now It Costs

The time will surely come for us
Now held back only due to circumvented throngs
To taste the bitter and the sweet
How long must we be pressed to pay for others wrongs?

You are always in my heart and mind
I wake to dreams only to find you're so far away
These dreams though make me realize
The value of what is truly good least of all what we must pay.

For nothing good in life is free
So the worth of this shall far surpass what now it costs
Just know you're always here inside of me
Never let what's now been made be ever broken, torn or lost.

Your Path

What is it worth…
To battle strife as days go slowly past
To do what inside we know is right when in the end…
It's gone by oh so fast?

Is this for real…
This test we've taken on to overcome
Where once we knew the only truth
Why did we choose to leave from whence we've come?

Our road is long… to take in all scenes
Which now must so be played
To bring back balance so long now lost
Yet through only will shall it longer be delayed.

We must let go… of worldly snares
That now our souls have bound
Turn back to self where lies were forged
And so shall your path be surely found.

Demise Of Dreams

Your journey has but just began
Though you feel your wisdom exceeds your years
The tests of time you've always lost
Revealing confusions poured out tears

At such an age where I recall
The world was mine though how I failed
My anger got the best of me
And demise of dreams has so prevailed

Take not all encounters in such light
For the aim is but to test your will
Remember all I've told you of what's right
And the integral thoughts I try so to instill

For thought this is just a passing through
We have got to learn our lesson well
Lest we'll return for one more try
To endure this self evading hell.

That Tear

What whispers on the wind as now I drift…
So deep in thought and what to do
Bring back the scent so soft so sweet…
Comes back to me…this essence just of you
When so much in love it seems so far…
Yet feels like only yesterday
When tears came to my eyes in fear of loss of you…
That tear so fell when you did go away.

I Only Want

I only want to hear you say…
That you're as happy now as when with me
Are you doing what you want and without fear…
That what you do he'll see?
I only want to know for sure…
That you can be for real in all you do.
Are you pretending, trying to fool yourself
By letting him think you love him too?
I only want to look you in the eyes
Because you couldn't lie to me…not now!
Because I'd see right through the mask
And if you lie you know I'll know somehow
I only want to know you see…
Because we made such promises to keep
Do you think I have at all forgotten this
Or was love shared so shallow…where it seemed so deep?
I only want to hold you once…
That I may know your love is gone for real
Is that the way of things from where you are?
Am I in love in vain…why is that how I feel?
I only want the truth you see…
But you seem oh so scared to give it.
Is this because you know how our love can be?
Well, it that's so, let go…come back now and live it.

What Will It Matter?

What is my love but just a word if there is nobody that will feel?
What is my life if spent in vain but so much less than real?
What is this life here all about that has us all confused?
What lesson learned is any good if never it is used?
What will it matter anyway if no one else can see?
What good is giving all my love if you're not loving me?
Am I to chase you through this life in hope that soon you'll care?
Or should I let you go your way and just keep you in my prayer?

Only What I Am

I can't make you dance on moon beams
But I can hold you in my arms
I can't promise to fulfill your dreams
But I can offer you my charms
I can't offer you much money
But I will never let you down
I can't promise all is sunny
But I'll always be around
I can't make the world a better place
But I can do all that I can
But I can make a smile be on your face
By being only what I am
I can't give you what I haven't got
But there's one thing I'll always give
That's my love for you and I have a lot
As long as we shall live.

Who Makes Me Right

It seems so far so many miles and sometimes feels so cold
And though our love I'm sure is strong time makes most things grow old
You have to feel me when I come to you when night is full
For I reach so deep to feel your love to make such pain grow dull
I try to call but you're not there how I wish to hear your voice
So as the chances now arise I'm left with little choice
You're such an anchor in my life as wretched as you may be
You are the one who makes me right the one who makes me see
So as I try to one more time I hope to catch you home
For without your voice to comfort me I feel so lost and so alone
But if you are not there right now I'll reach out just one more time
For if I can not hold you girl I'll hold you in my mind
For you're the one who makes me right and you'll probably always bee
The one who makes me feel so chained And at the same time sets me free.

Don t Let This Pass

Don't let this pass this chance to have again the
Pleasures and happiness together once we shared
Though time has hurt in many ways us both
We still remember how each of us so cared
And all the money in the world couldn't change my mind
Or how I really feel
Nor could no other no matter who
Deny this love for you
Which is oh so real
So don't let this go and leave the rest of time
To wonder what
It may or not have brought for how we love and what we make it now Is
ours to decide if we like it or not

Nothing Like It Really Seems

Don't let them take you down, stand up
You'll get subdued my friend
If you let these bastards shut you up

So know now it's not nothing like it really seems
they fill our children full of lies
fulfilling only their own wildest dreams

It's just a slavery trap to suck us in
I know from my own experience
This is the way it is and that's how it has been

Stand up right now let not their plan prevail
lest the doors to their trap close
And leave us feeling trapped and fragile

It's up to us, you see, nobody else will do
So stand up for what's real and right
And see this all the way through

And blood may spill but if it's right
then what we gain not lose
Will be well worth all the fight

Don't wait, my friends, stand up right now
And tell these bureaucrats
Where they can stick it when and how

Stand up, you may not think alone you're much
Don't believe it for one minute
And don't ever for the cause lose touch.

Its All Crap

I've heard so much and it's all crap
Even those that mean so much in the end just show me it's a trap
I've been lied to since I was young
Seems like I'd be use to all this shit
And know where everyone is coming from
But I guess I'm weak and it's all true
They see me coming or they wouldn't do
These things that they now do
Well, guess again, I'm not the one
I'll take no more from you
And know from now it's really on!
I'll put you to the test and you will fail
Because in the end so few will still hang in and will prevail
And those still left will see what's real
Because of all the hurt they've known
And all the love they've tried to feel
Well, know this now and stop your lies
And know I'm not the one with
Who all your bullshit now flies
Cause when you come to look so deep
You'll realize promises broke are ones you'll wish you did so keep
As off alone I walk and there you'll stand
Tell me now really is this the way you had it planned?

Its All So Hard

It's so hard at times just not to falter
When all seems lost and so far away
When you think you would rather sell your soul for fodder
Than deal with games so many play
It's not a life which you would always carry
The way you do if it was just your choice
But all it's weight makes you seem so wary
That now it's hard at times to even find your voice
You've put so much on love and lost it
Yet back again through loves door you'll go
And the times you know you just should have tossed it
But one things kept you clinging to what's real you know
And if when this life has really ended
And it is true of what some people say
Then all the efforts which you've expended
Will be rewarded come that final day
So walk the walk as others weaken
And hold your head with pride so high
And know this truth of which I'm speaking
Is yours alone and none can deny
If this you do with good intentions
Then at least you'll feel better of your own pride
To know you've beat mans cheap inventions
And evils trials you've now denied.

Fair To Feel

I've known more pain than it is fair to feel
And just when it's getting better or so I think
Somebody brings me back to what's really real
A world of hat and tromping on one another's toes
To hear from those you thought could understand
That's just the way it really goes
Well, let me tell you now I'll never bend
And have to deal with all the pain
And the condemnation in the end
So if you must get weak then just get on
I cannot condone those actions
Even if it means it's me alone
I love you so much, my friend, you see
Or may be I'll just say
I love the friend you use to be
But remember now that weakness kills
It may raise your social stature
But you're the butt of their cheap thrills
It's not too late now but don't think too long
For with the passing of a day
True love may have been but may have just gone
And if it's really love and truth you seek
Then hold your head back up
And walk the words you use to speak.

My Wreck

Yes, you're a wreck. How well we know
You seem so unaware
The things you do to hurt yourself
It seems you do not care
Yes, you're a wreck, how true indeed
And sometimes even worse
You tear the world around you down
Though your destruction must come first
You're such a wreck, and now I see
These warnings gave were true
But you're my wreck, so what the heck
What else can I now do?

My Family

Through all the years since I was small so much indeed has changed
And now though later than once thought
And not like once arranged
I look to you and where I'm at
And from where my thoughts first came
And I know that though we're different
Deep down we're still the same
Though not as close as I would like
And that's all due to me
And though very much has changed I doubt
You'll never really see
I love you both with all my heart
And yes I always will
At any time for either one
I'd die, if need be kill
You're more than just someone I know
Yes, so much more you see
And more than just my mom and dad
You are my family
And though our names be different
The only dad is you
You've taught me more than anyone
Inside I know it's true
And you, my mother, have been there
Where others would have run
And made me see where I was wrong
When all is said and done.
So just remember, mom and dad
You're always in my mind
And will be there eternally
Whatever fate I find
And though at times it's not so clear
It always is to me
I'd never trade for no one else
You're my only family.

Am I

What now will come since you are gone
What is in store for me?
Am I to live in such pain for long
Or am I to be set free?
Am I to choose the way I go
Or will the way be shown?
Am I to help in other ways?
I wish this all was known
Am I to be the one today
That does the things known right?
Or carries out the evil deeds
By darkness of the night?
Am I the one that you have chose?
Am I the one and why?
That seeks to find this entity
That fills the world with lies
Am I the one that now must do
What others here won't dare?
Am I the one cause no one else
Is left that seems to care?
And if I am the one indeed
Am I the one who'll win?
Or not in hell for eternity
For right that turned to sin

I Thought I Knew

I really thought I knew you well
But I knew you not at all
For every time I rest on you
You shift and let me fall
And I have kept this up too long
I can't go on no more
You say it's cause I'm far away
I don't think that's what it's for
You've grown so use to hurting things
From being hurt yourself, you see
You just don't know another way
Or maybe you'd stop hurting me
And everyone thinks I'm a fool
If back to you I go
And knowing how it really is
I have to say it's so
So excuse me while I stay right here
And have more time to think
Before I am a fool once more
And my ship again you sink
For my love for you is so much
More than you have known before
And my heart is not yet healed it seems
For it still is oh so sore
If you really love me like you say
Then it's so easy now to show
So think real hard and love me true
Or just let this whole thing go.

Finally Free

The time is ticking down right now
The dawn draws near for you
When you'll be walking down this hall
For the last time yes it's true
You've drawn your hand and played it out
Your days were numbered then
And now that time has finally come
You fade out remembering when
You fought for twenty years and now
The time has finally come
The price is paid all chips were laid
With the rising of the sun
You've had much time to think it through
These things for which you pay
Awaiting this the final day
As closer to the door you come
Your heart begins to race
"Don't make me go" your mind cries out
As the last door you now face
You thought you'd meet this consequence
With much dignity and pride
And now it's time to make that walk
You wish that you could hide
Yes, years ago you killed someone
And at last you finally see
The only fear to you as great
Is that now you're finally free.

Final Stand

It started oh so long ago in a place so far away
The Creator of all we now know
Got bored and went to play
He hung the planets in the air
And lit them with the sun
And then made gods to run all this
It all seemed like such fun
And then he made the animals
And the fish inside the sea
And birds that fly up in the sky
And then man like you and me
He gave them all a mate to keep
So this would carry on
Except the gods that ruled all things
And they felt so all alone
And they found favor in the brides
That now their selves would take
And once the seed to them implant
The giants of us did make but things
Stopped working out as planned
And they were banished from the earth
Except for those who hid too well
And were cursed for giving birth
There were thirteen to be exact
That were left among us here
And twelve that formed those ancient tribes
But the thirteenth which all men feared
His seed was of the strongest one
That was left here long ago
And he vowed he'd take the highest place
And his power all would know
And through the centuries it seems

His seed has filtered through
And parts of him are every where
It's bad but yes it's true
And now the time has finally come
For this show down to take place and the voice cofuses all those good
In hope they'll fall from grace
The two that carry power now
To keep good inside us all
He's separated with his lies
To make so many fall

Justice Be Denied

Such works before my eyes
But nobody will take heed
If soon they do not reunite
Then his evil will succeed
So hear me now, oh special one
You must protect this child it's true
And you've been right, yes all along
And the rest is up to you
I got you close and gave my love
And knew that this would come
And they have worked to push apart
This power known to some
And it is sad cause you can't see
They're right before your eyes
They draw you in and then confuse
Make you believe their lies
Now they have driven you from me
And I feel my purpose fade
And until you see and reunite
Our dues cannot be paid
And we are here to fight this one
That threatens all that's good
So take control my guiding light
I'll protect you like I should
You have the power to win this war
And if my hand you take
We'll find the path to do what's right
And his evil spell we'll break
And if you chose to turn away
For fear of what may be

Then I guess I'll just give in myself
For what good is only me
For you're the one that has been sought
To take this final stand
And it's not me that's mapped this course
And inside you understand
Don't let the fears from what they've done
Now push your faith aside
That's why I'm here to aid your strength
Lest justice be denied
The job is tough yes I admit
And the worst may still befall
But it's our job to do what's right
For the sake of good and all

Loving Only You

It seems so many years ago though really just a few
When things were looking only up
And I was loving only you
And then we vowed that we would keep together till the end
And felt no matter what would come
Together life we'd spend
And then it came that tragic day
We lost someone we loved
The Lord took him above
When I look back and try to see
Just what was right and wrong
It seems I can't stop loving you
And in the distance hear that song
And yes I acted wrong indeed
What else was I to do?
I couldn't bear the thought you see
Without the love from you
I guess it's sort of suicide
To hurt myself this way
But it's nothing like the pain I felt
Once your love had turned away
So to live the edge is what I do
To cover pain so deep inside
From love I miss so very much
And pain I try to hide
I swore I would love only you
That day those words were said
So stop wondering why I am this way
For I will love you till I'm dead.

So Much Has Passed

I sit here with you every night
Though you're so far from me
I take my spirit to your side
During this time I'm so free
I know that time can change so much
But inside I'll always know
That loving you as I now do
This love will never go,
I do not know just what it is
That you now want me to do
I pray each night for you to see
How I want again to be with you
And like I said so much has passed
Now I'm not sure I even feel
The love you use to send my way
Was love I knew was real
And though you say you love me still
Sometimes it's so hard to tell
You'll make me love you with your way
Then you'll made my life pure hell
And I won't ask for you to change
And if our love is now too late
Then let me know and let me go
And I'll see it's just my fate
Just know I sit here every night
And no matter what you do
I'll never stop the way I feel
And won't stop loving you.

I Must Be Blind

I can't believe I was so blind
That I refuse to see
How stupid do I feel right now?
To think that you loved me
And I so thought that all along
Your love for me was true
Why should I be so different
That you'd change the things you do
You've never thought to look inside
And see how others feel
Or you would know that what you've done
So many hearts have killed
How can you be so cold inside
To say that it's alright
To be with someone else today
And pretend to love tonight
You couldn't love or even know
Or you would see the pain
That you have put inside my heart
That makes this whole thing seem so vain
And now I can't begin to see
What it is I'm thinking in my heart
With you I'm still in love.
I must be blind to let us part.

I Hope The Best

I found you wandering so alone
And knew I had found a friend
And you reached out and touched my heart
And made my love for you begin
And then both had dues to pay
And still were so confused
Because of all the hurt gone by
All the times we'd both been used
But I broke down as I did feel
This love for you so strong
And hoped and prayed for this to be
The one to last so long
And after all the dues were done
Or at least that's what we thought
We loved so hard and loved so good
Till that day we finally fought
And yes things did get in the way
And took control you see
But not the things that you conceived
For all love was yours from me
And then you went away so far
And I have not been right since then
I sit and think and dream of you
And how good it once had been
And now good it once had been
And now the chance has come again
For us to try it one more time
And I love you so very much
I hope you will still be mine
But if you choose to turn around and let love slip away
I hope the best for you, my love
To come to you some day.

Back From The Stars

Like unicorns and purple rain
And trips beyond the stars
Or images that dance at night
Seeming closer than they are
Your love for me at times eludes
And I sometimes cannot see
That though I missed the train to mars
Our love is what must be
I let you have your way it's true
And if you crash or fail
I know that when I pick you up
Our love it will prevail
You're such a special soul you are
I know that's why I stay
Because if I used logic at all
It wouldn't last a day
You make me know what real love is
Both high and low extremes
And sometimes I must stop and ask
If you know what loving means
But once you come back from the stars
And on my chest you lie
I thank the Lord for sending you
And hope to keep you till I die.

Where Stardust Falls

The places traveled by us now
Forlorn as they may be
Where moonbeams dance with unicorns
For only us to see.
Are shared each night as others go
To places of their own
But I reach out to be with you
Together all alone.
Weve been apart, so far away
And many days it's true
But prisons walls can never keep
My soul away from you
The angels take me where you are
Where golden stardust falls
And I can be with you at night
Beyond these crippling walls
And though I can not kiss your lips
I smile when I am there
Though physically so far away
My spirits so aware
And as I wake my smile may fade
Cause I am not with you
I know the prison walls won't stop
These things that still I do
I'll keep on traveling as I sleep
To meet among the stars
And take my leave and love to you
Beyond these prison bars.

The Final Price

The heavens hold so much indeed
What are these answers that we need?
To at last go on to that final place
To rest before we go insane
We cope the best that we know how
And are bidding of our past right now
And hope to choose the road that's right
To go on one square and end this plight
And time is friendly if it's good
If you do life the way you should
But if you don't then shame to you
For any evils you may do
So think before you go to sleep
The company sought from dreams so deep
Or you may make a choice in hast
That causes that much time to waste
For time cannot you ere regain
It takes so much good to pay for pain
So draw what's good you know to heart
Lest one more time you'll have to start
And through this one more time must go
Till all's achieved that you must know
Be careful, time won't pass again
Lest death be the final price for sin.

To Me Be Your Disguise

As I wait once move for night to fall
So again my life renewed
From victims blood upon my hands
Their own energy subdued

When daylight comes this need abates
And no longer comes the urge
To taste the blood and see the face
As in death do they submerge

I feel the power within me rise
As together we do meld
From death of them to life of mine
The rush like none I've felt

And as the night comes toward its end
I know now I must flee
What is this hideous thing I feel
Now rising out of me

I know that I must flee and fast
Or consequence be too great
For they will think they will be mine
And then shall seal my fate

Go from me now you demon damned
Leave me as sun does rise
And don't return again till dark
To me be your disguise.

Where No One Cares

I must undo the evil here
Before it is too late
And now's the time to intervene
To evoke to them my hate
They came like whispers in the night
And filtered through us all
And now the seed is sown alright
And the worlds began to fall
Rebuke the ones that house this seed
Remove their hearts and minds
So no longer will I feel the need
That I've chosen now to find
They're not from here, they've traveled far
To breed with us and live
Lest they should die on yonder star
That life will now not give
They look like us so be aware
Next time you choose a mate
Cause evil lurks where no one cares
And extinction is their fate
So if they work into your life
And find a place to stay
Don't be surprised when this your life
Turns to something else some day.

Just Your Paranoia

It's just your paranoia
Is that how you perceive
A world that's out to get us all
It's real, is what I believe
It's just your paranoia
That has caused you such despair
And even though they're out to get you
Doesn't mean they do not care
It's just your paranoia
That has finally driven you away
Now you can't see what's real or not
And how I'm who now must pay
It's just your paranoia
And I hope you sleep and soon
So I can hold you once again
And put an end to certain doom
It's just your paranoia
That you must now overcome
And let me back inside of you
Where it's safe for me to run.

The Songs They Sing

Why do I listen to this voice
That leads me where I have no choice?
But to right the wrongs as they are seen
Take out the scum and those unclean
OUR world is now is such a state
It must be soon or be too late
For they now have plans for eyes that see
The things their minds want us to be
Imprisoned souls to do their deeds
If not stopped soon they shall succeed
The songs they sing to fool our youth
To me shows such substantial proof
That if we let them take too many more
There be none left to even the score
Take up the arms if now you must
Remembering only in God to trust
Cause when years from now from in a cage
Your heart is beaten from such rage
To think you could have set things right
If you would have just stood up to fight.

Beyond Reproach

We've been through all of this before
And know that it is true
That we will get it right someday
For that's what we're here to do
And both the forces pull at us
And try our minds to sway
So that our souls won't be at peace
When come the final days
And plans were laid so long ago
But the choice is ours to make
Which side we choose is strictly ours
And there's so very much at stake
And though what's right is hard to do
If we do as we all speak
But we tend to let the worldly things
Step in and make us weak
And life's so rough, yes this is true
If you be what you should be
And beyond reproach from others stay
For all the world to see
So above all else remember friend
In all things you shall do
The judgement that will come to pass
Lies on no one else, just you.

Seek First The Spirit

Seek first the spirit in your life
And know the purpose of your deed
Make love and truth be what motivates
Be aware of all which may impede

For merely thoughts they so may seem
A single thought may change your fate
To cause trouble never like foreseen…
Or to make what's wrong turn to what's great

What's in you heart, when spells are cast
Is what will for sure come back to you
So send with truth all you put out…
And with love do what you must do

For the soul perceives the heart of man
Thus evolves back from whence did start
No longer gods…the master plan…
And with love do what you must impart

For we were cast by light from God
Sent out to make amends for wrong
So back someday we all could come
To merge and form a love so strong.

Shattered Dreams

Subliminal implications call to me in the night
Aware of distant times so long ago
Knowing when you're in my arms, it all seems very right
This familiarity of centuries gone which both we know

We have both been through this so many times it seems
But still we just can't seem to find the way
So well tear it down one more time to wake to shattered dreams
That pride and fear alone again have pushed away

I'll try once more to love you when again I am awake
For to turn my back would kill me now I know
So come on lets end the shattered dreams the chance again to take
So our love can be fulfilled as it does grow.

Our Special Dreams

These clandestine situations have now so increased my sorrow...
By bringing out charades of this now so twisted fate
As I cling to sleep afraid to wake and what shall come tomorrow

I'll fight back the voice that warns me so...that it is far too late.
What once we shared with reverence it now seems you've put aside... to
achieve such purpose as I cannot comprehend
You say that you so love me, yet have so many times denied
Your love to me is sacred yet to others you pretend

You have lived enough to know the truth but still you live a lie
I can't go on here any longer hearing what you have to say
For to have you in my arms again would be worth all the tears I cry
But I can't go on without your love another day

So as I say farewell to you my love, it's best now we do part
I have counted sorrows far too many or so it seems
Just think of me and love we shared know you're always in my heart
In some other world we'll meet again, if not just in our special dreams.

Counted Sorrows

I just can't believe what's going on
No...not in a million years
What was oh so right could not turn wrong
Where once were only smiles, are tears

We counted sorrows by the score...
Until the day we chanced to try
For we knew our love was so much more
Love so intense is for to die

Still death...I'd welcome any time
Now that you've gone from me
To be robbed of your love is such a crime
For which my heart won't be set free

You will always be my queen of hearts
Until the sands of time do fade
However far we are cast apart
All counted sorrows shall be paid.

Your Only Knight

With the dawn returns reality
As no I come from distant worlds
Bringing back to me mortality
My spirit gathers from whence unfurled

I've battled for you to the death
Not just in dreams but times before
Always to love until dying breath
To die for you and so much more

I'll always be your only knight…
Yes! You shall always be my queen
Protecting you to me seems right
Since before all time that's how it's been

So if you should dream of dragons doom
But wake without me at your side
Know in my heart there's always room
Your knight, my queen, never denied.

Both Deceived

The dark has overtaken me
And through the hours I'll fight my foes
Knowing in my heart you'll be,
If I shall endure these sorrowed throes.

You left me when I needed still
The comfort felt from love received
I cannot believe to be your will
The pain we've suffered both deceived

We told of love we wished to share
And yet were fearful of patterned truth
Now we both know how swift the snare
Can catch us sleeping our lives the proof

When I do wake I hope someday
That again we share what now seems lost
For we both know what's gone today
Should be returned at any cost.

Superficial Whims

What God has made let not be spoiled...
By superficial whims of selfish mortality
For centuries untold have we so toiled
Through this quest for higher spirituality

When so focused on a point is light...
All else becomes a blurred mirage
And what does emerge if it's not right
When does return...is hard to dodge.

For what once was again shall be
Prophetic dreams have said this so
So restrain what you would want not to see
Come back so we shall once more know.

Engulfing Love

From so far away does to me come
Engulfing love from days long past
A bond not known by most, but some
Which eternally shall surely last

When others drift off to no avail
Your warmth of love touches my soul
To know you'll be there without fail
To bring back what's real and make me whole

For oft as not, though scattered be...
Your caring brings back to me the light
So where once was blinded, now can see
Giving hope that what is wrong will right!
Our paths have crossed since time began
And this I know deep in my heart
We have both covered as the other ran
To be free of tares and regain new start

If you ever need...you know I'm there
It matters not what burdens laid
For there burdens not where love and care
Is given rather than is paid.

Let Me In

Let me in, my fair maiden,
Lest I shall surely die so lonely from a broken heart
I know not why so surely now
That I let things go or let forever let us part
Come back I cry into the black of night
As I chase you so vainly among the most twinkling of stars
But you seem so to elude me with your angelic wings
First so near oh then over so far
I am your knight and have been so forever
And so if alone I must die then is that must just be
For there is only one maiden for this knight
And that surely is you you're the only queen I'll ever see.

The Mountains Have All Washed Away

We use to dance among the starts
And climb those mountains just we could find
We once were satisfied with this
It gave us both such peace of mind
But now the starts have lost their luster
And the mountains have all washed away
And every minute I'm not with you
Makes any time just another day
You made my world seem oh so special
By being part of what was me
The fact that I was blinded badly
Is because I just refused to see
So now I search my dreams so vainly
No stars to light my paths so dark
No climbing mountains with you, my lover
The dreams I hold now have no spark
Come back to visit if you dare to
Come take my hand and again let's dance
Come one more time you won't be sorry
For ever having took the chance.

Brothers At Arms

Shoulder to shoulder…stood the three
It wasn't heart they lacked
Brothers at arms eternally
They had each others back

Some may call it suicide
There'd be no turning back
More a matter of personal pride
Too much balls too little sack

Their end marks the beginning
Of masterpeace unfurled
Call it the bottom of the first inning
And the shot heard round the world

Kipling, Poe or Robert Frost
Could not have said it better
Yet the true meaning remains
Like my wife in Dolly's sweater

Poems of trees or Gun-Ga-Din
Or words of never more
Cast your stone only if you've not sinned
The Raven's at your door.

Hathaleague, hathaleague, hathaleague on…
Rode the fearless three
Free at last they will be done
Grateful and dead like Jerry G.

"Edgar Allen Bo"

Cast Out Your Word

Is this the cost so set aside…
For me to pay for wrong to you?
My love you now have so denied
Is this justice…these things now you do?

To know my heart is held to your fate…
Shall you allow for dues so paid?
How can you so long make me wait
To only have this sentence stayed?

Cast out your word that I shall know…
Will you return what's so revered?
If not in solitude I shall then go
As now for so long I have feared.

This Torrential Tide

My life…now held inside your hands.
I must tell all from in my heart
Of mice and me and those best laid plans
Of which now you are so much a part

My freedom once more has been denied
And I've now washed upon your beach
Be careful of this torrential tide…
It tries so to put me out of reach.

I know I should not rock the ship…
When at the mercy of such waves
Hold firm my friend…lest I shall slip
And again be cast amongst the slaves

I'm trusting you that you may see
That wrongs inflicted are not my crime
Yet crimes of those empowered be
Those never paid…by loss of time

To pay when owed is just and right
But for me to pay where debt is NOT
Is worth all I am and I shall fight
Never more shall these things be forgot

From Where Now Comes My Fear

You took part of my soul…
On the day you went away
Feeling so much less than whole
Like a night that will no more see day.

With you I felt so complete…
Like a purpose had been fulfilled
The taste is bitter where once was sweet
Such sorrow to me you've instilled

You told me you wouldn't do it…
But you did it anyway
Knocked down all I had, and knew it
Nothing has changed now but yesterday.

Don't think it will be so good…
If you come back for one more try.
I know better now like before I should
It's not so easy now to make me cry.

I think you better keep your place…
It won't be like you want it here
No…I don't live at your pace
So know from where now comes my fear

V
Sorrow Of Situation

These two things are come unto thee; who shall be sorry for thee?
desolation, and destruction, and the famine, and the sword by whom shall I
comfort thee? Isaiah 51:19

Dizzy, my dopey dwarf

I really was not going to do this because I really think it's rather
condescending to my demeanor at the present time.
However, Mrs. Stinson, it bereaves me to consort certain ambiguities
concerning the dispensation of our foregone preeminent cohabitation.
One of the predicaments I am having perfunctory paranoia about
presumable peripherates phrom my phear of personally produced pedicure
procedures. It comes to my attention that you have successfully sustained
surprisingly superior substantive, subcutaneous savvy. I believe you've
hereby sort of situational stymied strenuous steps sought to secure sanctity
and alternately avoid screwing off severely my most sedulous spirituality.
At present this leaves me prone to pillage amongst the peasants provided
pectoral perspicuity as well as perverse psychotic personification of
pfemales is provided.
If not I concur in this conclusion that I cannot cope with constant crust
on the cuticle of my corns. So cordially confiscate the cash to cajole a
conveyance to California before my callousness cavorts my celf to cill you.

Lovingly yours,

Well you know!

Terminal Reality

Our terminal reality... extends itself to flank full force,
To remind us once again of what must come
Though subjected spiritually... reminds us of our right of choice
That separates the integrity of most from some.

This so repeated circumstance... reveals its purpose,
thus enables us to rise or to descend,
Yet even further to resist but still residual redundancy... sometimes holds
us from our earned prize by putting principal
where feeling should not exist.

Rising in repulsion...From so many wrongs, never made right,
Have brought us back here once again to make amends
And my contested compensations...
make me fight off these demons in the right
And wait for time to come that this nightmare too shall end.

Destined Born To Lose

It seems so damned hard for me to just stop loving you
You have gone away and turned your back so many times on me
Still I can think of nothing, anytime I would not do...
If still I could have one more chance to let this again be

I've often felt I'd rather die than be kept from you another day
Still inside my heart I know this is just another lie
As long as there is life in me for the chance I'll always pray
Knowing never was there love as good, so tears for you I'll always cry.

It hurts too much to hear your voice, it makes it hard for me to speak
Still I must tell you how much your loss has taken all my life away
When you tell me you still love me, it makes my knees grow very weak
Yet I know inside my heart that this is just the game you play.

I've given in to what is now to be the path I'm forced to choose
Other choices take me down roads without you, and I'd rather just not go
So now I face the cold hard fact that this time I am so Destined, Born to Lose
I'll now go through life without your love, and hope so much it doesn't show

All Dragons Gone

Unfolds from melted dreams…
So long since past emerges now desires retained
How long shall muddled deceit so last
Till justice head rears…rights so long gained?

In solemn twilight turns the tide
And quest is filled…again to go
This end result, never to hide…
For knowledge held from long ago.

What's now put off shall come again
For wrongs shall right, before all wanes
The price be paid for all past sin…
All dragons gone shall then be slain

Though price is high…all must be done
No turning back when cause is met
For paid by sacrifice for what shall come
Is worth far more than paid as yet

Chosen Of The Few

From whence travels come…to now this day of dawning
When all eyes shall see, and shall so be made aware
This time to wake…wait no longer, for no lots we'll be drawing
It's only those that let go burdensome grief…yet remains the tare

Of these shall be the chosen of the few, to lead us ever on
To right these wrongs…which have now kept us so enslaved
Lest we shall too be left to wonder…as all once ours is gone
For that none would follow…yet now cry out so to be saved

Not many knights remain…that will so put their honor on the line
For those not known…yet cause be motive for this their noble deed
Cry not oh children…it is not your place to pay for now past crime
Go gallantly these chosen of the few…let not dark forces your quest impede

For you all were cast as those so long ago…as souls of living light
Your purpose here, and worth to all is far beyond compare
So shine in causes battles…to bring once more day from night
Go now the chosen of the few…where only you, yet no others dare

To Look Without

Deeds done...from lives so long since past to reach this point through
destined doors
From gods...our souls so far were cast
Goes whence, till now, as well the mores

In fury laden, all were cast out... to find again that so long now lost to take
all evil...and all doubt
The purchase shall redeem the cost.

This encounter...though seems to be so long is but a grain in sands of time
To pay with right what's been so wrong
What must first come then self to find

To attain the right to look without... must first come truth and peace within
Then all that's gone shall come about
No more the wage of long past sin.

What Snares Are Born

It matters not what fate has now placed upon your path
But only that with love of heart and internal guidance you proceed
For to look beyond what snares are born and reach for the light
And know what shall be given in love and faith is all you need.

If you can look into yourself and pass all of your once felt doubt
And can do out of love what once was done for only self
You have then opened up the first of many doors surely to come
Which house more than any shown by this know worldly wealth.

It's all but a journey back from where we all have been to become one
again of that which cast our souls from same
For to become whole and know that we have earned this right is to put
behind this life and be glad to be a soul not just a name.

He is despised and rejected of men; a man of sorrows and acquainted with
grief: and as we hid our faces from him; he was despised and we esteemed
him not. Isaiah 53:3

Come On Now, Baby

Come on now, Baby…
It's time to stop playing games now
You've got to let me know somehow
If you really love me
Or is it over… if it is then I will go my way
no longer this game can I play.
It hurts to bad, don't you see?
It's been a long, long time and it's not done yet
No matter how I try I still can't forget
The way I feel when I hold…don't you know?
I have lost so much in so little time
Can't you see I'm about to lose my mind?
Baby, why did you ever have to go?
Come on now Baby…
I can feel you reaching to love me
I know that pride won't let you see,
That I'm so lost without you
So stop your lying
To yourself as well as to so many others
You know that never another,
Will make you feel like I do.
You are so far away won't you come back home
So I won't be destined now to die alone.
You hold my heart in your hands so don't let go
I'm so hurt inside that I can not see
Don't you know that your love is all there is to me?
So what do I have to do before you'll know?
Come on now, Baby, this Desperados destined to love you.
I'll put no other above you, if you'll just come home to me.
I love you so much. And I'd rather die than be without you
So come on and love the one who loves you too
Before it's too late, can't you see?

Jaded Dreams

Your psychotic ebullition eludes your most jaded dreams...
Bringing back to you realities of this chaotic life you live
You may find yourself encumbered by the wrath of all your schemes, so
much in fact you feel put out by what little you do give

Your ecstasy excites your soul, as dominion comes to you
You use your vengeance as a fallacy in your mind to justify
You claim to be so righteous, still, yet nothing right you do...
And if your life sustained on truth, you'd surely die.

Livid when confronted, by the truth of how you are...
You turn from what's real, and right, to run away
Afraid to know what real love is, you have ran so very far
Though I should let you go. I love you more with every passing day.

Don't be so hard on those you love, it really need not be
Be honest with those hearts you have to keep
Know always that my love is more and only you can see
For you are with me all my waking hours as well as while I sleep

No Place Left

So many days have now gone past
Since it was I saw you last
Now nothing wants to go my way
I have not anything more left to pay
You have taken all there is of me
Then you left me here alone to see
That love is such a wicked lonely game
Without you…life's just not the same
And God won't even let me die
Although I ask so often…why?
He turns away just as you've done
Now there's no place left for me to run
You have made me feel so empty now inside
Is there no place left for me to hide?
I won't let go of dreams of you
You'll go with me in all I do
So maybe someday you will know
How much I lost when you did go.

Come Down From There

Come down from there my friend…
Do you not surely by now see
That no matter what you know inside
Nobody else will let it be.
Come down.

Come down from there I beg of you
Lest you should die from cold of rain
Or from the heat of scorching sun
Cannot you feel the pain?
Come down.

Come down from there my final plea
What is this presence of which you speak?
Are you the only one who can see
Are all the other eyes too weak?
Come down.

Cone down I ask before too late
And they come to haul you far away
Because you so insist they're there
Come sleep now, return another day.
Come down.

Only You

I was just feeling kind of lonely really wishing you were here
Instead of where our lives have led us growing farther is my fear
I have never known another that could bring me down so far.
Just by thinking of our memories and wondering how you really are
I know you're not one that will beg me and you are probably just fine.
But I wish so we were together that once again you should be mine.
For I'm so tired of being lonely,
No, there's not much that couldn't be
If once again I'd feel your heartbeat from being oh so close to me.
So if the time should come for you now
When again you're lonely too
Know I am here and will be always forever loving only you!

I ll Always Be A Friend

I'll now say bye to you, my friend though I must say it's not right.
That you'll go out the way you are and not put up a fight
You cannot see the forest, babe because of all the trees
Someday you'll wish that you had looked before you made your peace
You want from me something, my love that I can never give
The lies that you insist are true are the ones we can't relive
You've went and turned your back on me and look where you have turned
back to those who made you hurt and made sure your soul was burned
And now that you have let me go I hope for you all good
As I would try myself to give To you, it, I just could
Please don't forget the good we had and I will do the same
But don't accuse me of something where I shouldn't be at blame
I loved you as a friend, you see before I let you in
So if you must then walk away but I'll always be a friend.

Then should I yet have comfort: yea, I would harden myself in sorrow: for
I have not concealed the words of the Holy One.
Job 6:10

IV
Sorrow Of Humility

And Hannah answered and said, No my Lord, I am a woman of a sorrowful spirit: I have drunk neither wine, nor strong drink, but have poured out my soul before the Lord. I Samuel 1:15

Just as it says, it's hard to swallow pride and face humility and become humbled before God and man. I've dedicated a lot of this section for my friend Genel for obvious reasons from the precluded verse known only to us.

I love you, Genel, and you are always in my heart.

Here's to inside synonymous jokes, eh?

Slow Down

Let not your hubris impede your pace
Make this mortal joust be your benefaction
Slow down…realization you soon must face
To attain these planes of earned satisfaction

Pride is the hardest snare to defeat
In this quest to attain substantial light
Being humble, true, and without conceit
Are essentials so needed to get it right

So as now you go keep this in mind
Send forth from thine heart, as you wish received
Through all these things, someday you'll find
It's vastly greater than ever you've perceived

Celestial Repression

Malice with intensity... reaches out and grabs my soul
As I now fight these flashbacks in my dreams.

Suppressing animosity... from other lives, lived long ago.
Subconscious recall, makes time shorter than it seems.

Oppressed obsession... now calls to me, from so very far away, as I recall
the pain from love, lost many times.

Celestial repression...Hold memories motives, still at bay.
Yet leaves me thinking love was taken for past crimes

Unconditioned servitude...
Holds you captive in my heart,
From love instilled so many times I dare not say.

Intermittent solitude... and all the miles we're now apart,
Makes me so wonder, how much longer must we pay?

Wipe The Tears

Wipe the tears…
Wipe the tears away, my love.
The time to cry is gone.
So wipe now the tears from your face.
Though these walls encompass us my love…
Wipe away the tears
No longer shall we fear the pain,
For now we've found true love.
So wipe the tears…
Wipe the tears out of your life.
Replace them with loves smiles.
Wipe away the tears,
Wipe the tears.

Don't Change That Dial

Do not attempt to change the dials
It is no use, you see
This world in which you find yourself
Is from now on, how it shall be
The days are gone where you can say
I know him like myself
That's what has urged you after all
To take the guns down from the shelf.
The ones that you so loved it seems
Will be the first to go
For deeds so evil in your eyes
That you never thought you'd know
They tell you of a life so good
And tell you how to live
And take till nothings left of you
And still want you to give
So do not attempt to change the dials
You're stuck here, don't you know
There's no where that you can escape
There's nowhere left to go.

Ripples

Some say a thought is just a ripple
And all that will be once has past
And love if sent out to another
Is the strongest spell that's ever cast.

And I believe that things are destined
But fate is in the hands who know
And let the pieces fall to places
That open up the way to go.

All things are linked by things in common
If not from here then from before
And once the path has been discovered
Then keys fall and unlock these doors.

So if you find a path and like it
Then do not let it lead you wrong
And you will be the better for it
If not then let it make you strong.

For somewhere that door again will be
In front of you again to choose
And if driven by light, love and goodness
By choosing it you'll never lose.

And when in this life the road has ended
If you have found you place to be
Let it be known to those you love
So they choose and too will see.

There's More To It

It's so much more, this life we live,
But who's to say what's planned?
Throughout the years, so many ask
And still don't understand.
You've made me stop and think it's true
How short life here will be
And now it matters in the least,
Unless you are here with me.
I'll never love another, see
The ways that I love you.
For you are always in my heart
No matter what I do.
So if you feel there's more to it
Than it does sometimes seem
Then know my love will outlive life
And that this is not a dream.

Smiles Turned To Tears

I had a dream the other night and you were sitting by my side.
This made me happy yes indeed because you were to be my bride.
I had a smile upon my face that none could ever wipe away.
Then came the part I had forgot when you did leave on that sad day.
The dream resumed but it had changed and now I was no longer glad
For smiles had turned to tears, you see and my good had surely gone to bad.
And then a ray of hope shone through and put a twinkle in my eye
I caught a twinge of hope you see as you did smile while passing by.
I knew inside I loved you so and not anyone could fill your place
Nor would the smile be in my heart until once more I saw your face.
So now I drift back off to sleep and hope to wake someday to you
For if I don't I'll never smile no matter what I choose to do!

Prisoner To Your Heart

To be away for oh so very long...
Ah yes, but how the mind forgets
Those times past all that were wrong
why must you feel now so much pain
Where should be felt so much regret.
To be so much a fool must be a crime...
To feel so much a prisoner to your heart
How can you still fight after so much time
And surely still not see and not refrain
Knowing what will come but still you let it start
To ever really know how pain can be...
The worst is in the heart
And in also the mind
But until it is too late oh never will we see
The wisdom so long ago we should have obtained
So peace, my friend, should not now be hard to find.

Sweet Sorrows!

This urgent need…
To feel your lips on mine
To taste so of your love…
Sweet sorrows so divine.

Come back now…
Don't flee - once more for to be gone
In this the waking hour…
Surely darker, is to me the dawn.

Such pleasant times…
While dreams of you surround
Partaking of each others love…
So distant any sound.

Such sorrow comes…
Alone to wake, so sad it seems
Driving me to push my life…
To recapture you, inside my dreams.

Love Hard

What is this now, what have you done to me
Or is it only fault of mine... for eyes too love blinded to see?
The past can't change and pain from sorrows slow to heal
But strength derived from love over pain is so very much more real
I open up my heart in hopes that you will know my path
For destined is my soul to you so come close, dear, loosen thy wrath
We both loved hard and knew the stakes were surely high
So love hard so tears will we no more have to cry.

Walk That Walk

No more shall I break down, get weak.
You've made me see, oh yes indeed
I should have practiced as I did speak.
I'd have left you there with lightning speed
I trusted all the things you said
How this and that are suppose to be
God should have just struck me so dead
Instead he blinded what I should see
You surely know just what to talk
To sway me so your trap would close
Too bad you didn't walk that walk
Too bad for me your bait I chose
For now I am the one who pays
And you must surely have a laugh
To know the pain you dealt still stays
You caught me napping, I'll give you that
But you can bet no more you'll see me fall for lies from one like you
For I know what inside I'll be
And know not what you say you'll do!

Time For Everything

There is a time for everything
At least so many say
For loving, hating, hurting, healing
And all happen in many ways
A time to cry, a time to laugh
And at times just be alone
To find new paths which you can take
For better days to come
I hope this time I've found a friend
That will not let me down
That with the good as well as bad
Will always be around
I often wonder why myself
That things go like they do
But I thank all the universe
For the chance of meeting you.

Tears Of Blood

You talk of love to me...on what authority?
How dare you think you even qualify.
For you don't know how to love you see...
Only how to knock down walls with your lies
And I've been such a fool! This now too late
I know that I'd even listen to another line, I should be shot
But not so simple as that could it be.
No look what a show as you sit and laugh, to see the pain I from you got.
I only hope you're happy now because you're killing me
And you act like you could never,
nor have you cared
What do you do, turn the other way so not to see?
For I could not watch another's pain, not even dare
My heart cries tears of blood from pain
of your love and pain that can't be seen but surely will not die
I ask to have your love back to God so great above
So I can stop this masquerade and no more cry.

Without A Sign!

Without a sign to let me see,
You torture my heart so.
Not knowing where you now may be
Nor which way should I go
I do not understand at all
These feeling now that will not pass
My knees they weaken, wish to stall
Such sorrow shall not surely last
Hoping soon you'll be where you belong
Yes at my side forever more.
Lest I should have to be so strong
But why without you what is it for?
I beg you now, come back my world
For the universe so empty seems.
Like shooting stars through space are hurled
Past everything burned out their dreams
My heart it stings from loss of you
My life is empty motions now
Come back my love, I beg you too
So will to live, comes back some how.

Just Because You're Paranoid

Though you may surely see them not…
You feel their presence all the same
Never will they to you reveal their plot
Nor even will you know their game
You feel their eyes where they can't be
Because they see from far away
So mind things you'd have not them see
For in the end it's you who'll pay
Don't ever think they aren't there
Oh for they follow close indeed
But when you turn to see their face
They disappear with such great speed
Yes, just because you're paranoid
Don't ever think they won't get you
They even know your every thought
It doesn't matter what you do
But don't go tell you know they're here
Or locked away you'll surely be.
Because the one's you choose to tell
Are the ones they'll never let them see.

Hope For Dawn

Again I rise alone
Why must this hurt so much
And just the absence of your touch
Make clouds appear inside
Where once the sun so shone.

I somehow move along
To find the joy I knew so gone
But still I dream in hope for dawn
To bring you back to me
To make right what now seems wrong.

Again I go to sleep
In hope beside you I will wake
If not my soul pray God
To take to ease the pain I know
Lest again I have to weep.

I Won't Let Go!

These walls may keep us far apart
But never can they stop our dreams
Where we can share each others space
And things can be just how they seem
I'll ask you not to give your heart
But just your hand, now come along.
And we will share inside our dreams
What others sing of just in songs.
We'll climb those mountains if you like
Or we can drift among the stars.
No matter what you want to do
Come take my hand now as you are.
I will not let you go, you see
So don't be afraid, I won't let go.
Come share these special dreams with me
To those places only we will know.

To Be A Fool

Why must I feel the pain I do
Tell me would you please
Because I chose to so love you
You shall drive me to my knees
To feel so much less a man today
For giving all my heart to you
Now to feel the sorrows here to stay
How much more shall you to me do.
If I could just get back the pride
And face again the day
Without having what I was denied
For you being just this way
You let me down more don't you see
By hiding from what's real
And not telling only truth to me
Not making known what you do feel
I thought you to be so much more
But I see now I was oh so wrong
To be a fool and look what for
This pain has lasted way to long.

IV
Sorrows Of Mind

And the ransomed of the Lord shall return, and come to Zion with the
songs and everlasting joy upon their heads: they shall obtain joy and
gladness, and sorrow and sighing shall flee away.
Isaiah 35:10

I am, as all that know me quite persistent in my 'causes' in life and believe
firmly if you obtain the proper degree of faith, and exert the proper
amount of patience…Like Mary's little lamb they'll all come home and
be all the wiser for their sorrows of hearts and mind both interred and
inflicted, wagging their little tails behind them.
Seana…You've Been a Bad Girl!

Queen Of Spades

You gave such purpose to my life
And I fell in love so much with you
I played into your hand too far
But didn't bluff as so you do.
The chips fell on the table fast
I even borrowed just to call
But drew off to an inside straight
You made me fold and took it all
Now never will I draw a card
In life's came if it involves a queen
For though the queen of hearts she looks
The queen of spades she's always been
And I once thought that I could play
But never have I seen such stakes
And she will win most every time
The best of them their heart she breaks.

Intensified Love

I feel this pressing need intensify…
The need to fill desires to regain life.
This thirst so great for wine to me…
So sweet to drink so of your fluid of my greed.

This love I feel for you will never die…
Nor shall your soul, however condemned it be
This choice through passions cry…
Feeling the strife of this a world that has to fight to stay alive.

We must live in this incubus, which we can only know
Till our desires do we fulfill, again to grow
This passion shared of life from death
To taste of blood once more…and take last breath

To live on till need does come
Again to take what must we to sustain
This life we masque though dead
We've always been animated by those who's life we now obtain

Behind A Mask

Why must things be this way...
Are not we free...
Are we so blind to the ties that bind...
That we can't see
Nor do we know shy we must pay?

Do we so pay and rob ourselves...
Or hide the feelings...
That we should share it is not my choice...
Nor is it fair to keep our love upon a shelf?

Is it just destined not to be...
Because we chose too soon...
Is it too late or is it wrong...
Or surely just our fate so others cannot surely see?

Will we be able to stop I ask...
Or want to if we could...
Would you, or would you not...
What will we do, hide love behind a mask?

My Prison Cell

What's this now that I feel…
From loss of you…such emptiness.
Oh how though can your absence be
Or pain so deep…more than the sea.
But which to me is oh so real?

Shall this not surely some day pass…
How shall I live…with so much grief
And know that you'll no more return
For just one more day in hell I'd burn
If that day left me smiles to last?

What now I ask could be more…
The pain from loss…of destined love,
Or to burn from fires of my own hell
My heart to be my prison cell…
Without you, what's it for?

I Wonder

I wonder what you're thinking now
Are you missing me like I do you?
Are you still in love a bit at least
Can you feel the things I do?
I've missed you so and hope you see
The things I've come to know
Your absence love has made me learn
How I want our love again to grow
I know that time can't change the past
But we can change what is
And you will know once in my arms
From that moment when we kiss
I hope that this has also let you see
That you are still my world
Cause without you its not the same
I'm so lost without my girl
I hope that you can find the truth
That I am trying to show
Because you are all there is to me
And I hope this lets you know
I'll never let a thing in life
Again between us come
Because I'd rather die I think
Than to ever have my heart so numb
I'll be here for you faithfully
Yes each and every day
To be your friend and so much more
At least for this I pray
You mean much more to me you see
Than you must even know and once you realize this you see
You'll never want to go!

When I Awake!

I can feel your breath upon my lips
And your passion fills my very soul
As I embrace you once again
And love we shared again controls.

From passions heat my heart does race
And though I may try I can't escape
You have me in you spell once more
This agony must be my fate.

And oh so real the touch of you it
Drives me mad because I know
When I awake this love so real likewise
With this dream too shall go!

Transcendental Torturer

My transcendental torturer... you are so wicked in your ways
Never caring what's inflicted, but to you.

Your astral apparitions... haunt my nights and fill my days
With so much loathing for the thoughts of what you do

Still your intermittent innocence... gets you through life's sudden snares
You walk away unscathed where dearly others have to pay

Your disparaged dispensation... has never answered many prayers
So I must grit my teeth to hold my rage at bay.

This paranoid preponderance... puts this pain inside my soul
It will no perish till again you are with me.

Your eminence encapsulates...I am so much less than whole
Yet you're so blinded by your ego you can't see.

Caught In Emotion

I don't know where this is going...
I've waited so long for some sign of what is to come
Impending fear in me growing...
Patience to me is not a virtue, like it is to some.

I can't help what I'm now believing...
You feel so far off, it's like you will never return.
Yet still your words are deceiving...
Inside my soul, for your love I so desperately yearn

I can't get rid of this feeling...
That keeps me chasing you endlessly now in my sleep.
Can't you see how I'm not dealing...
With all those promises, Baby, which now you don't keep.

I'm so caught up in emotions...
I cannot tell you in words just how badly I feel
Though I still can't shake this notion...
That my love for you was ever anything less than for real.

Yes, I'm so caught in emotion...
You've got me where I just don't know what to do.
But I've come now to this conclusion...
Life isn't worth anything, unless I live it with you.

I Won't Give In

Just give up you say, stay weak, they've got you now… and you have no
place left that you can turn?
I won't give in to their trickery, NO NOT me! I'd rather lose life than to
go out that way, knowing in hell of my own I'll burn.
What right have to think, let alone say, I should lie down… and let them
have their way…win one more round?
Because once more I've quit, did not stand up and fight… knowing my
cause is right, and you'd have me not make a sound?
Not me! No more you'll see. For now to me it's not a game.
It's my life they're playing with, not just a number in a slot.
For what…to fill a need, sustain further their greed? I'll just stay!
I won't play…not just so someone else must pay…I will Not!
So look around. I say to you…you fool…yes! I damn sure do object and
NO! you're not so cool…to say that I should let them win.
To me…this the end…only will justify the means in weak minds and if ever
it does it will be because I've won if right. Not how it's been
So you can do down…for something so wrong…but by yourself and then
I'll believe the things you preached, not ever more.
For I've been put under their gun when right, too many times it seems and
now I know…that you truly can't see, what I am fighting for
For I'm fighting not for me, but those too young, who know not what to
do and those children who've been blinded and can't see,
what more is yet to come
I must try…to open now their eyes and ears…and put the fear in them
away so they shall be let to speak out for themselves,
lest not know from what they run.

See! the face they wear, to you it smiles, but it's venom you can't see
For to choose them over the ones you love it surely is a crime.
I can't believe they hypnotize you thought…To hear you say…
But they are right! How can this come from your mouth, surely not your mind
You are the ones who taught me "it would be okay!" Well, its not… and I've
tried your way. Look what I got, for admitting wrong when right.
NO! I really don't think so! I'm more a man you see than you do think
For I would rather die now than to lie down for them without a fight.

Why Do I Keep Standing Up?

Does it really matter now,
Who's right or wrong at all?
Is it worth the hurt inside us both
To see who'll be last to fall?

You may not even know for sure
What started all this fuss.
But I know what I am feeling here
Is too much for both of us.

I love you far too much you see
To let you fall from here.
But I don't know how to catch you
Or if I should even dare.

So why do I keep standing up
Just to have you knock me down?
Well at least this way I guess I know
That you are still around.

Epilogue

In the forty years and some that I have graced this planet with my rather encumbering existence, I have gained a lot of experience and knowledge. This has helped as well as hindered me in my path toward the higher spiritual consciousness that we all need to achieve.

I believe that all things happen for a reason and if we recognize and act with the proper responses, our paths become less littered by physical, as well as spiritual obstacles.

However...being as I am and acting as I often do, my pride and ego become my major stumbling block in my journey. Thus creating even more sorrows, though they be somewhat self inflicted, that I must endure.

The poems that were written in this book are feeling that have come from love and hate, joy and sorrow, pleasure and pain, contentment and much confusion, that comes as part of being human

In my spare time, I like being a writer of sorts and though I have a long way to go to be anywhere near good, I enjoy it.

I'd like to share something of a somewhat personal nature especially with the younger people out there.

I have four beautiful daughters, all of whom I can see a lot of myself in, not only in the physical, but in their actions and thought patterns as well. I lost a son in a rafting accident several years ago and as a result, I've beat myself up pretty good for it. As also I have drowned in sorrows many times for many reasons.

I was in the drug scent trying to bury the pain and have hurt several people unconsciously in fear of getting too close only to lose again.

I have now been clean and sober of the street drug and alcohol scene for quite a bit of time and I know from experience that it doesn't matter how deep you bury yourself, you have to learn the lesson that the situational cards of life have dealt to you, this is all part of achieving total spiritual enlightenment.

I chose a Bible verse as an excerpt on my introduction and title page for each section. I have done so for several reasons. One being that my grandmother has told me all my life I had a purpose here and that if I live right and have faith, God would lead me the right way. Well, maybe that's most of it. I also believe, however, that if we look inward and discover God and self and learn to dissuade as well as merge when necessary we will progress as meant to from the beginning of time.

I use to think drugs were a pretty good cover for everything, but as I now progress I know that they open the door for too many negative forces and only hinder the long run.

So think long and hard when you get down to the level of killing the pain. Seek shelter instead within, for we were all cast from the light of God and every soul is a part of that eternal light so to seek God first, seek self. Turn inward and be at peace.

Know that much pain is for selfish reasons and when you put the selfishness aside and become selfless, good things will come. Maybe they will take a day to come or may be several years, even a lifetime or two or three, but keep the faith and do what you do in the right spirit.

This book is dedicated mostly to the memory of my son, Jason Allen Miller. I know God is graced with your company as we all were and though you are not physically with us you are forever in our hearts.

To my Grandmother. Granny, thank you. I know that this red hair gave you many fits when I was younger, but I'm getting it...I think!

To Mom and Dad. I don't have to say for what, that would cover a few novels. Just thanks for everything...most of all for believing in me for so many years.

To Kim 'Lil TAZ' Miller, my all-star girl...stay bold for Dad.

To Courtney Miller, my brain child. Thank you for leading us all through a lot with your wisdom of situation and the ability to rise above it all.

To Seana, 'my curse'...well, 'you've been a bad girl!' I'll love you forever.

To Genel. Thanks for being there, when nobody else was. I love you for many reasons through and thick or thin, you are the foremost.

To Jim. I love you, brother. Let's go fishing and have a beer to tainted love and Harley Davidsons.

And last, but certainly not least, Robert 'Bo' Hicks, my lead Brother at Arms'. STAND UP! You've inspired that 'keep them in power in check' attitude in me and guess what...I wanna be...you got it! ANARCHY! Viva la Revelucion they ain't right!

Thank you, my readers. I hope you have a smile, a tear, a laugh and one of those 'spinal rushes' from knowing where something I've written comes from. I love you all.

Thank you very much.

For I have satiated the weary soul
and I have replenished every sorrowful soul.

Jeremiah 31:25

The End Of Vol.II

The sorrows of death encompassed me and the floods of ungodly men
made me afraid.   Psalm 18:4

Made in the USA
Coppell, TX
28 March 2021